Realer Than Reel

REALER THAN REEL
Global Directions in Documentary

BY DAVID HOGARTH

University of Texas Press ◆ Austin

Requests for permission to reproduce material from
this work should be sent to:
  Permissions
  University of Texas Press
  P.O. Box 7819
  Austin, TX 78713-7819
  www.utexas.edu/utpress/about/bpermission.html

⊚ The paper used in this book meets the minimum
requirements of ANSI/NISO Z39.48-1992 (R1997)
(Permanence of Paper).

Library of Congress Cataloging-in-Publication Data

Hogarth, David, 1959–
    Realer than reel : global directions in documentary /
by David Hogarth. — 1st ed.
        p.   cm.
    Includes bibliographical references and index.

        ISBN 0-292-71260-X (pbk. : alk. paper)

    1. Documentary films—History and criticism.
I. Title.
PN1995.9.D6H56   2006
070.1'8—dc22
                                              2005011657

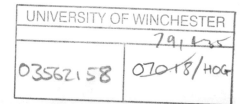

To my families and friends and,
of course, Brigitte

Contents

Preface **ix**

1. Introduction **1**

2. Documentary in a Global Market **19**

3. Global Documentary and Place **41**

4. Global Documentary and Public Issues **62**

5. Global Documentary and Meaning **92**

6. Digital Documentary **122**

   Notes **137**

   Selected Bibliography **171**

   Index **179**

Preface

We often hear that we are living in a post-documentary age. This is a time when audiovisual truths and the ways we perceive them are fundamentally transformed by new types of cultural mediation and reflexivity. For the most part these claims are made with reference to particular presentation styles, modes of address, and actuality claims in particular texts from particular countries, mostly in Europe and North America.

In this book I want to make a similar claim, though somewhat differently. That is, I want to consider how documentary has changed, but not just with reference to texts, and certainly not just with reference to texts from particular places or cultures. *Realer Than Reel: Global Directions in Documentary* is a study of the transnational political economy of documentary and its impact on production, viewers, and documentary discourses. My particular interest is in the way places and public issues are meaningfully represented in export-oriented projects and what this tells us about documentary and global culture generally.

Readers will note that I am concerned with documentary in the broadest sense and particularly with documentaries that are often seen as "cross-overs" or even bastardizations. This approach is deliberate. I devote much of my attention here to reality shows, nature programs, and the like partly because they are seen by so many people in so many places, but also because as "limit cases" they help shed light on the issues I am concerned with. I reject fixed, exclusivist definitions of the genre that have guided so many documentary studies to date, and I (critically) engage mainstream markets and mainstream productions with no apologies.

I also focus here on documentary television and the various networks by which it is distributed around the world. Television, I argue, has become documentary's principal medium and global broadcast networks its biggest producers, changing the genre quite fundamentally for the foreseeable future in most parts of the world. As critics, it is time for us to acknowledge that fact, however much we may pine for the cinematic styles and standards that guided the genre for nearly a century.

Finally and naturally enough, I am mostly concerned with global documentaries—with productions designed for export markets or at least with export markets in mind. I am certainly aware of the arguments that documentary (and television in general) is national by nature—nurtured by national public service cultures and destined for viewers in national markets. But on balance I believe contemporary documentaries are decisively shaped by global capital flows to the extent that they are neither channeled nor contained in predictable territories in predictable ways with predictable consequences. This is the main theme of the book.

What follows started out as a series of conversations with students at York University, Toronto, Ontario, where I teach courses in international communication and television. It grew in scope and scale after further talks with colleagues in Toronto and Montreal. And it took final shape with the help of families and friends from around the world, especially Ben and Dolores Locicero. I thank all the above for their support, and most of all my partner, Brigitte.

Realer Than Reel

ONE

Introduction

By many accounts, these are either the best or worst of times for documentary and ultimately for its chief medium, global television. For the editors at *Television Business International*, the world is being swept by a wave of "documania"—by an unprecedented volume and velocity of real-life images that inform viewers about world affairs as never before.[1] For veteran director Albert Maysles, on the other hand, global television is suffering from a glut of "McDocumentaries"—standardized factual products offering few aesthetic surprises and no political punch, serving to fill "500 factual channels with nothing on."[2] This book assesses documentary as a genre and global television as a medium in light of these debates. It is organized as a study of nature and history shows, public affairs investigations, the "first person" real-life experiences featured in British and Australian "docusoaps," and the "staged but real" events showcased by American-style reality programs. In this book I examine variations of these genres around the world, focusing on their ability to represent places and public issues in meaningful and coherent ways.

Realer Than Reel: Global Directions in Documentary is principally designed to raise questions about documentary in a period of global and televisual transition. Documentary's factual authority, for instance, may become uncertain in the wake of digital manipulation techniques on the part of global producers and new modes of "aesthetic reflexivity" on the part of global audiences.[3] In the same way, documentary authorship and point of view may have to be reconceived in the wake of series production and multimarket programming practices. Similarly, documentary aesthetics may become "postcinematic" as sounds and images are produced on video for high-definition TV screens around the world. Finally, documentary's relationship with other genres may shift and blur as programs are produced, promoted, and distributed in increasingly "nondocumentary" ways. In short, this book begins with the observation that documentary must be rethought as a generic category in a global televisual age.

But documentary itself can also tell us something about global television. If television today is really best understood as a "homogenous, meaningless fantasy factory,"[4] a genre traditionally dedicated to the representation of places and public issues in more or less orderly ways would appear to be either a public service hangover or a market anomaly at best.[5] A study of documania thus allows us to question, in a grounded and empirical way, conventional wisdom concerning local representation, free speech, and meaning in a contemporary televisual universe. It lets us investigate, that is, the ability of global television to document places and issues of collective importance for citizen-viewers around the world. This book is thus designed as an up-to-date critical assessment of documentary and the medium that carries it within and across borders. As in these preliminary comments, my intent throughout this study is to ask what has happened to documentary and what this tells us about television today.

Documentary as Film

Perhaps we should first take a look at documentary and the broad structural changes it has undergone in recent years. How, specifically, are factual sounds and images produced in new ways, and how has the genre evolved since its "Golden Age"—since its days as a form of public service cinema for the nation-state?

To begin with, documentary can be said to involve an entirely new medium and project—specifically the production of entertainment-oriented, mostly commercial programming for television. It was not always this way. As is well known, the public service documentary tradition—the tradition with which most documentary studies are still concerned—involved the production of factual films mostly unconcerned with immediate appeal or profit, designed to inform viewers about the world in which they lived. Film itself was an integral part of the plan. As productions, publicly supported factual films were seen to encourage diverse images and ideas, more or less free of the assembly-line compromises of broadcast culture. As texts, documentary films were seen to allow for formal experimentation and rigorous factual argument. And as viewing experiences, documentary films were seen to elicit the sort of dedicated, undivided attention by which mass audiences might be transformed into educated citizenries. Productions of this sort were supported by national film services around the world, particularly in Europe and areas influenced by it, from the 1930s to the present.[6]

Documentary thus had its roots in twentieth-century notions of filmmaking and public life. Canada's National Film Board documentaries were exemplary in this respect. From the 1940s to the 1980s, NFB productions took anywhere from six months to six years to complete, according to former director Sidney Newman.[7] They varied in style and substance depending on the complexity of their subjects and the approach of their filmmakers. And they tackled weighty social issues in an effort to provoke thought and even action on the part of citizen-viewers. Documentary filmmaking was thus largely conceived as a collective and specifically national cultural project.

Of course, these productions never encompassed documentary everywhere at every time. Throughout the twentieth century, many documentarists concerned themselves with formal and avant-garde experimentation rather than staid, civic-minded documentation per se. At the same time, many public service producers were less serious or sober than Golden Age accounts suggest, with nature filmmakers, for instance, often deliberately shocking and entertaining viewers, particularly in the broadcast sector.[8] Finally, and crucially, viewers rarely responded to documentary messages in predictably public ways, at least not on a widespread or regular basis as far as we know.[9] In short, documentary was always something more than civic-minded cinema. But be that as it may, it seems fair to say that filmic public service was the genre's dominant guiding principle, subscribed to in theory if not practice by producers, policy makers, and pundits around the world, from the beginning to the latter part of the twentieth century.

Documentary as Television

This makes recent changes to the genre all the more remarkable. In a word, documentary has been radically televisualized in recent years, giving rise to modes of production and consumption quite at odds with those described above.

The signs of televisualization itself are everywhere. In Europe, 94 percent of documentary funding now comes from broadcasters, domestic or foreign.[10] In the United States, television money is nearly as dominant, often undermining various modes of cinematic and online distribution.[11] And around the world, documentary investors look beyond cinema, with just one of thirty-seven recent RealScreen production workshops concerning itself with film distribution per se.[12]

Televisualization in turn has entirely transformed the prac-

tices and pleasures of documentary as we knew it. In the televisual era, for instance, documentary production has largely
broken with filmic modes of craftsmanship and public service.
It may be unfair to call today's factual programs "McDocumentaries" with all the low-culture connotations that term carries.
But for the most part, broadcast productions are quickly and
cheaply produced compared with their filmic counterparts,
often undermining a single producer's vision along the way.
Unlike national cinema institutions, production markets like
the specialty channels generally seek efficiently predictable
factual products that build a brand image and fill a lineup (see
chapter 4). They tend to commission series installments rather
than stand-alone features (see chapter 5). And they usually
pay rock-bottom license fees that encourage producers to co-
produce with numerous partners for different markets (see
chapter 3).

At the same time, these productions may compromise authorial integrity in entirely new ways. Certainly few documentary programs involve the imposition of a personal vision on
an inviolable text (see chapter 2). Even fewer can be regarded as
"authentic" projects of a single, grounded artistic creator. With
productions routinely "co-ventured" and "re-versioned" for
multiple markets, most of them concerned with broadcasting,
notions of authorial control are increasingly subject to question. It is perhaps a sign of the times that the world's largest
programmer in this area, Discovery Communications, plans
to stop screening producer credits at the end of its shows, arguably making documentaries more anonymous than ever in
the global broadcasting business. Indeed, one early observer's
"shock" at "how little a director's work was considered" at a
1979 MIP world television market now seems almost quaint
for its auteuristic concern.[13]

As documentary production has changed, so have documentary texts. Clearly, factual sounds, images, and graphics have
been fundamentally reworked for television markets, even if
there is little precise agreement on what these changes have involved. For some critics, television produces flat, standardized

texts; French cultural theorist Felix Guattari derides an obsession with meaning and "semiotic order."[14] For more conventional public service advocates, television offers up "depthless" documentaries in which linear (and often lengthy) arguments are compromised by commercial interruptions and frivolous recaps. And for postmodern observers, television encourages genre-blurring and even semiotic disorder on the margins and in the mainstream (insofar as we can still distinguish them). It is true, as I will argue, that the "television effect" on documentary has been both more profound and less predictable than these models imply (see chapter 5). But critics are right to say that television has decisively changed the way factual images are packaged and produced.

Finally, documentary reception has to be reconceived in a televisual age and again in fundamental ways. The very structure of a documentary program—that is, the often incoherent mix of commercial interruptions, internal and external narratives, and direct and indirect modes of address—may lead viewers to engage with programs in a cooler, more detached way than traditional cinematic models of audiences suggest. Theories of textual interpellation, for instance—themselves subject to question in contemporary film theory[15]—hardly explain the power and the pleasure of broadcast documentary. Certainly, a collage of sights, sounds, and styles—the overall documentary intake of a single night's multichannel viewing —hardly qualifies as a coherent diegetic space where a straightforward process of "identity formation" can take place. At the same time, a juxtaposition of documentary styles (insofar as it exists in most television schedules) may encourage a degree of critical distance on the part of viewers, undermining traditional notions of documentary authority along the way. Questions concerning the factual foundation of reality television and docu-animation can be seen as examples of this type of "aesthetic reflexivity," which seems to be both widespread (among critics and laypeople) and worldwide (see chapter 5) in scope. Again, in all these ways television requires us to rethink documentary, and from the ground up.

Documentary as Public Service Broadcasting

Clearly then, television tells us something about documentaries. But what do documentaries tell us about television? For instance, how have documentaries helped define systems and structures of broadcasting? And how specifically has the genre shaped and reshaped the medium that delivers it to viewers around the world?

Documentaries have shaped television in a number of ways. To begin with, factual programs in the documentary tradition have helped constitute public service broadcasting as we know it. It is not just that documentary television has been incidentally associated with the effort to represent events and issues in various parts of the world—there is more to it than that. Indeed, in the last half-century, documentary programs have introduced public service technologies such as videotape, color television, and digital broadcasting, which have recorded various aspects of the national life particularly in Europe and North America. They have helped create and define the discourses by which public broadcasters address national publics. And they have come to embody a dominant social realist aesthetic by which fact and fiction programs have been judged for truth and occasionally beauty.[16]

Of course many documentaries have fallen well short of these ideals, but the genre's overall contribution to public service programming has been undeniable. In Britain, documentary programs are seen to exemplify the BBC's ability to inform and entertain a national audience.[17] In Singapore, they "nurture an intelligent and discriminating public."[18] And in Canada, they demonstrate the Canadian Broadcasting Corporation's ability to produce "high impact programming" that reaches audiences as citizens.[19] Around the world then, documentary is seen as a public service bellwether—and even more importantly as a test of the nation's ability to represent itself to itself in a world without borders (see chapter 4). It is fundamentally in this sense that documentary remains a signature piece of national public service culture in a global age.[20]

Documentary as Market Commodity

But there is another way of looking at documentary, a way that again requires us to rethink if not repudiate many of the public service assumptions which have guided its theory and practice for nearly a century. That is, aside from showing citizen-viewers life as it is or should be, documentaries serve to make money for their handlers, both domestic and foreign, around the world. For better or worse, documentary programs are increasingly produced and exchanged for profit within and across borders, independent of any easily discerned national "cultural" mandate. In part then, documentary must be regarded as a transnational commodity that tells us a good deal about commercial as well as public service culture in a global age.

On the face of it, this way of looking at things seems much less plausible than the first. To begin with, the arguments against global market television, documentary or otherwise, are compelling and varied. Curran, for instance, reminds us that most programs, factual and fictional, are produced "at home" for domestic markets.[21] By most accounts, audiences prefer local shows where they are available—which they are in most genres and in most places. A number of recent market studies support these conclusions, and we can only agree with the author's dismissal of earlier predictions that "most people, most places will be watching 'Dallas' or the Olympics at the same time."[22] Television, documentary or otherwise, shows no signs of going global, at least in a straightforward way.

Just as television has resisted globalization in the grand sense, it may have avoided the all-consuming commercialization process that goes with it. Public service television continues to dominate many broadcast territories, with many services dedicated to local culture first and global profits second. If people do not actually watch public channels, they may watch others with similar commitments, and much of their intake is guided by state regulations requiring, among other things, local information.[23]

In short, documentary programs seem to be a perfect, stubborn case of broadcast domesticity. Indeed, even economists who defend the idea of a global cultural market consider documentary to be outside of it. Programming of this type is generally seen to be burdened with a high "cultural discount"—that is, an inability to cross borders with market value intact.[24] At the most basic level, documentary's public service values—its concern with local places, local issues, and culturally specific ways of seeing—is seen to impede its ability to "travel." And if cultural economists have been wrong before—many assumed comedy would never travel well, for instance, until NBC's *The Cosby Show* became an international syndication hit[25]—the obstacles to border crossing seem insurmountable in documentary's case. Kilborn's (1996) observation that the genre still does best in isolated public service pockets[26] has been backed up by recent studies which suggest that, strictly defined, documentary has survived in Europe, parts of North America, Australia, and some of Asia and the Pacific Rim while disappearing in most of the rest of the world.[27]

Empirical research thus suggests that documentary is a place-bound, commercially inert genre—a stubborn anomaly in a global market age. Even recent worldwide corporate projects—such as the various offerings of the Discovery network—can be dismissed as specialty services in the most diminishing sense of the term. Transnational documentary channels, for instance, seem to attract much smaller audiences than their domestic competitors,[28] and many seem to operate as "duty" offerings that lend the cable and satellite services that carry them a much-needed public service veneer. For all these reasons, documentaries seem firmly grounded in the supportive terrain of local public service cultures. And as such, they seem to refute the existence of "post-national" television—at least as it has been conceived by its most exuberant market boosters.

But for all that, a closer look at documentary makes the idea of global television more credible, if more complex. First, statistics suggest that the worldwide market for documentaries is larger and healthier than most academic studies claim. Even if we exclude popularized documentary types such as reality television and docusoaps (which I will argue below we should not) the genre appears to account for at least 8 percent of the world television market, a sizable proportion compared with other seemingly more commercial categories such as quiz shows.[29] Industry studies further have predicted that between 1995 and 2005, television documentary production will have grown at an annual global rate of 8.3 percent by volume and 2.4 percent by value,[30] considerably above the industry average and probably an underestimate if one takes into account what other studies call the "seismic shock" of reality television on worldwide markets.[31]

Not only have critics underwritten documentary's market value, they seem to have underestimated its global implications. It is important to remember—as many documentary studies do not—that the global and the local are not easily kept separate in today's factual marketplace. For instance, "global" documentary programs that receive transnational financing for exhibition around the world are usually produced by local companies, regulated by national policy agencies, and consumed primarily by "home" audiences. But just as surely, "local" independent documentaries often receive commissions from global corporations and funding from foreign investors, after which they may be entirely revamped for "local" screenings abroad (see chapter 2).

Even historically grounded public service projects have been "globalized" to this extent. Recent cooperative ventures between national broadcasters like the BBC and global operators like Discovery, for instance, suggest not just a degree of rapprochement but a more transnational market outlook on the part of the former. Though public service channels still serve home territories, more and more look for profits in foreign markets, independently of any easily discerned local "cultural" mandate. Expanded coproduction and syndication ventures are two examples of this trend, but there are others (see chapter 4), and it is important to keep in mind that public service documentary must now be seen as something more than a national or even international project, conceived within or between nation-states. In fact, as we shall see, global markets and local cultures routinely collide in ways that compromise the integrity of each. It is in this ambivalent "glocal" sense that documentary has taken a global direction. That is, while documentary remains grounded in local and national markets around the world, the creation, distribution, and reception of the programs is no longer strictly contained within national borders. In short, documentary encourages us to question the lines and flows of cultural production today. And in this way it may tell us something about global culture and its ability to represent our worlds.

Documentary as Global Culture

But tell us what exactly? There are, in fact, several questions concerning global culture that documentary might help us address in specific terms. Perhaps most important, at least in terms of the critical attention it has received, is the issue of cultural homogenization—the fear, as Arjun Appadurai has put it, that overcoming physical distance will result in overcoming cultural distance within information networks.[32] In this view, places could look the same and eventually be the same, partly for want of proper documentary representation. For instance, globally circulating reality television formats could serve up homogeneous accounts of the "everyday everywhere"—dictated by standardized licensing arrangements and universal style guides (see chapter 3). Similarly, copycat nature shows could display generic flora and fauna, presented in a stultifying and ubiquitous American entertainment style (what one bemused Swedish producer calls the "feed, fuck, and kill formula").[33] Zygmunt Bauman's nightmare scenario of "everyone, everywhere . . . feed[ing] on McDonald's hamburgers and watch[ing] the latest made-for-TV docudrama" (or a glibly localized version thereof) seems to be in the making.[34]

Also at stake here is the ability of global documentaries to deal effectively with issues of collective concern. The ten-

dency of documentaries, particularly "dumbed down" commercial documentaries, to offer emotional first-person reports
that circumvent any form of logical empirical argument has
been the subject of much comment lately. So has an insularity
of output, with documentary producers and programmers al-
legedly taking little interest in affairs beyond their own market
borders (see chapter 4). Our question here is whether documentary has become a critically empty form incapable of dealing
with local and global public issues of the day.[35]

Finally, there remains the question of what global documentaries actually mean. Some observers have concerned themselves with issues of documentary coherence, that is, the ability of multiply authored, dispersed, and disorganized texts
to make sense of the world in more or less unified ways;
others have focused on facticity, that is, the ability of "post-
representational" infotainment forms to support the epistemological foundations on which documentary "truth" was built.
In both views, documentaries may be moving toward an amorphous "space" with few geographic and generic borders (see
chapter 5).

There are other issues concerning global documentary, but
these, it seems to me, are the outstanding ones. In this book
I consider whether and in what way factual images will continue to allow for documentation in a hard or even a soft sense.
And more specifically, I ask whether and in what ways global
television will continue to represent places and public issues.
In short, *Realer Than Reel* is concerned with the ways audiences around the world might understand and shape their lives
in years to come.

Global Documentary in Theory

In doing so, I hope this book breaks new ground. To begin
with, in *Realer Than Reel*, I deliberately focus on commercial and popular offerings particularly in the broadcast sector,
and in this sense it is somewhat of an anomaly. For Steven,

for instance, TV productions are barely worth considering because "new documentary," by its very definition, departs from "media-driven" formulas.[36] For Zimmermann, only public service shows merit attention because "critical [documentary] investigations" have all but disappeared from commercial television.[37] And for Roscoe, multicultural public service programs are interesting, but not domestic market shows that "play it safe."[38] Even Stella Bruzzi, who sets out to examine "contemporary and accessible" British documentaries, devotes only one chapter of six to television per se.[39] *Realer Than Reel*, by contrast, begins with the assumption that documentary should be scrutinized in the mainstream as well as the margins to better assess new types of local and public representation emerging in a global cultural marketplace (see chapters 3 and 4).

Further, the chapters that follow are specifically concerned with globalization, again at odds with the thrust of most documentary research. The few studies of global documentaries that do exist tend to be cursory and mostly abstract. Zimmermann's analysis of transnational market pressures, for instance, offers virtually no analysis of core institutions such as copyright regimes and coproductions.[40] Similarly, Longfellow's study of Canadian historical reenactment exports ignores global production and promotion patterns entirely.[41] In studies such as these, "real" documentary is still seen to emerge from the film circles of the nation-state. Here I focus on productions largely beyond these confines (see chapter 2).[42]

Finally, in *Realer Than Reel* I consider the importance of documentary for global culture, again at odds with most research in the field. Documentary is not even mentioned in Verna's survey of global communication, which takes the "Live Aid" broadcast of the 1980s as its paradigm text.[43] Similarly, Chris Barker's introduction to global television only considers news and live broadcasting as factual types.[44] Meanwhile, studies by Winston, Corner, and Kilborn and Izod focus mostly on national public service documentaries and the ways they have been affected by internal and external market forces.[45]

In short, transnational research is largely absent from documentary research, while documentary analysis is mostly nonexistent in work on global television. My intention here is to bring documentary research up to date and global media analysis down to earth (or at least down to cases) by focusing on the specific ways documentaries circulate within and beyond borders. This involves a sensitivity not just to multiple national contexts but to the penetration of those contexts by forces that are no longer, strictly speaking, national or even international in scope. It is these "global" televisual forces that are the focus of this book.

Documentary: A Global Approach

But the question remains: What sort of global forces and global documentaries should we be concerned with here? What is a "global" documentary anyway, and how should we study it? And what might a global approach to documentary look like? Here I want to argue for a broad-based, contextual way of proceeding.

First, I believe a global approach to documentary should involve a more open-ended view of the genre itself. That is, we should adopt a flexible definition of documentary to suit the social, cultural, economic, and technological circumstances in which it now operates. After all, if television calls into question cinematic theories and markets partly undermine conventional notions of public service and transnationalization challenges Eurocentric models of all these institutions, then a wide-ranging global understanding of documentary would seem to be not just appropriate but indispensable.

In practical terms, a global approach would begin by investigating so-called documentary "mutants" and transgressions. Rather than dismissing reality shows, for instance, as bastardizations of long-held documentary truths or the dumbing-down of conventional documentary styles or even the "sexing up" of traditional documentary program packages, a global approach would investigate the ways these shows may, under certain circumstances, be as natural, unstaged, and epistemologically secure as their national public service counterparts, as serious and socially engaged as conventional public affairs programming, and as sober and even self-important as the most pompous public service package. It is worth pointing out, for instance, that studies in France and the United States have noted a progressive blurring of documentary and reality TV substance and style, a trend that may become more pronounced as generic (and geographic) boundaries take new shapes.[46] Here I will argue (particularly in chapter 5) that documentary fringe forms can no longer be dismissed as simple counter types outside a "real" documentary corpus.[47]

Second, a global approach to documentary should consider new types of information concerning new types of programming—specifically information about markets, much of it coming from producers themselves. That is, just as we take into account a global range of documentaries, we should keep in mind the complex interrelations between these programs and the cultural, technological, and political-economic spaces in which they now operate. In other words, no matter how inclusive, textual analysis is not enough. A global approach should attend to the material as well as symbolic forces that give rise to documentaries in different contexts.

Again in practical terms, a global approach would view documentaries as something more than symptomatic texts—texts that tell us something about larger texts such as particular cultures or deep-seated social preoccupations, for instance. Instead, we should examine documentaries more broadly as contingent outcomes of particular technologies, budgets, and scheduling needs emerging in conjunction with broader cultural forces. To return to our old example, reality shows should be viewed not just as postmodern paradigms but as organizational artifacts—for instance, as lineup items that helped British public service programmers compete with their fiction-focused private counterparts[48] or marketing devices that allowed U.S. network producers to align new products with

new ads.[49] Programs like these—along with other documentary types—arguably reflect specific industrial conditions as
much as they do a broader zeitgeist. As such they remind us of
the need for contextual as well as textual study in global documentary analysis.

Finally, a global approach should pay more attention to
the testimony of cultural *producers* in various countries and
various markets. That is, if we are contextually concerned
with the ways economic, political, technological, and cultural-
textual forces come together to produce documentaries around
the world, then we should also attend to what I will call the
metadiscourses of the documentary market. Of course, this
involves paying attention to techno-forecasts, investment reports, and policy statements. But more, it requires that we concern ourselves with discourses about documentary discourse
that emerge from market as well as academic circles. Simply
put, documentary producers and handlers may have a good
deal to tell us about the conditions and consequences of their
work. After all, many practitioners regularly appear at theo-
retical sites such as festivals, forums, and conferences where
they must explain their work, and most of them work under
the scrutiny of cultural guardians, near and far, policing the
borders between information and entertainment, good taste
and bad, and the "authentic" and the "staged." For all these
reasons, documentary may have become a globally reflexive
practice—a practice that draws upon local and distant under-
standings to make documentaries differently (if in the most
incremental of ways). This makes the views of global documentary "agents" all the more worth attending to.

With these considerations in mind, this book examines a
wide range of documentaries from a number of perspectives.
Specifically, *Realer Than Reel* examines public affairs, nature,
and reality shows from around the world, drawing upon industry data, producer interviews, selective textual analyses,
and firsthand observations of market sites. These issues are ap-
proached from a number of points of view. Chapter 2 considers

documentary globalization through a region-by-region breakdown of market activity in Europe, the Americas, Asia, Australia, Pacific islands, and Africa, focusing on growing transnational links in the form of exports, co-ventures, and festival contacts. The chapter concludes with an examination of the global documentary channels serving these markets, providing a wide-ranging snapshot of documentary production today.

Chapter 3 takes a more conceptual tack, considering what documentaries tell us about the representation of place on global television. This discussion challenges the assertion that emerging "international styles" have made the genre largely incapable of dealing with the particularities of regions and locales and takes as its case study the "glocalization" strategies of Discovery Networks International, the National Geographic Channel, and France's Odyssey service. Recent regulatory efforts to impose domestic content quotas are examined in Europe, Australia, and Canada, along with producer initiatives to ensure local self-representation. The chapter concludes with a critique of the way "place" has been conceived in all of these discourses.

Chapter 4 considers whether and in what ways documentary programming will address its viewers as citizens. Issues of free speech and documentary diversity are considered in light of recent patterns of consolidated program distribution (by a small band of documentary super-channels) and "postfordist" specialized production (by a growing number of independent and semidependent producers). This discussion is followed by an examination of censorship, copyright laws, and various other restrictions on the free flow of documentary images across borders. Best- and worst-case scenarios of documentary public service are considered, based on an analysis of public service broadcasting in Canada, "diasporic" public programming in Europe, and reality television in a number of markets (including the migration of the *Survivor* series from Sweden to Britain to the United States). In light of this evidence and drawing on recent discussions concerning post-national public spheres, chapter 4 considers whether, as one critic puts it, "the space for documentary to explore difficult issues in far-away places is shrinking every year."[50]

Chapter 5 is concerned more broadly with documentary meaning in a global age. This discussion focuses on the supposed collapse of notions of facticity and taste, coherent viewing practices, and, indeed all temporal and spatial boundaries in factual program service. Chapter 5 examines digitalized production, channel zapping, and computer-assisted distribution in this light and concludes with a case study of hybrid docusoap programming around the world—where distinctions in conventional meaning have arguably collapsed while at the same time allowing for the reassertion of traditional (and often local) notions of facticity, sense, and taste.

Chapter 6 considers the future of documentary as a genre and television as a global factual medium, taking as its case study a new wave of documentary multimedia services being developed at CNN, PBS, and the BBC. This chapter, like the three preceding it, includes selective but in-depth analyses of national, public service, postmodern, and "post-televisual" texts. All of this material is designed to consider whether television will continue to "document" the world in any meaningful sense of the term.

TWO

Documentary in a Global Market

The Concept of Documentary Globalization

Is documentary moving in a global direction? This is a difficult question to answer for both empirical and conceptual reasons. To begin with, statistics concerning documentary often come in the form of proprietary research, which can be both inaccessible and unreliable. Further, data can be both overly general and overly specific: general because it concerns not just documentaries but factual programming (which can include anything from news to cooking shows); specific because it focuses on domestic markets, making transnational comparisons difficult. On top of all this, documentary is defined differently in various countries, making an accurate gauge of global production problematic if not impossible.[1]

Putting aside the big picture, globalization studies are hampered by a lack of grounded data at the domestic level. Few national sources provide a complete or accurate measure of documentary production in their own backyards, making even a cumulative study of documentary around the world a challenge. Balance of trade reports, for instance, generally provide little information regarding foreign investments and export revenues for factual television.[2] At same time, revenue studies tend to underestimate inflows and outflows, particularly in low-budget documentary sectors that generate more program hours than income.[3] Even the most balanced and comprehensive reports may be stymied by exporters' reluctance to fill out forms and disclose sensitive financial information.[4] In short, documentary exchanges leave few statistical traces, making empirical measures of documentary globalization problematic at best.

Conceptual matters further cloud the issue. That is, even if we did accurately gauge documentary inflows and outflows, we would still have to determine what they mean, what we might call their cultural significance. This is a tricky issue as consensus concerning the nature and impact of cultural globalization, let alone documentary globalization, is notably lacking. If by this term we mean the emergence of a worldwide meta-market where one type of audiovisual product reaches one worldwide audience, documentary globalization would probably entail a good degree of cultural uniformity and predictability. This would be the world Zygmunt Bauman spoke of, where everyone eats the same hamburger and watches the same docudrama[5]—presumably in a similar way, to the detriment of local culture everywhere. If on the other hand global culture involves a degree of what Tomlinson calls "complex connectivity,"[6] documentary globalization involves something else altogether—a much more fluid mediascape constituted by global flows of production resources and resulting in potentially hybrid or "rhizomatic" documentary markets around the world. Globalization, conceived this way, involves not just predictable cultural losses—a simple eclipse of local documentary filmmaking traditions, for instance—but also reflexive gains in the form of new documentary styles grounded in producers' knowledge of cultural practices beyond their own borders.

The Case against Documentary Globalization

Documentaries are almost certainly not global in the first sense. That is, nowhere and in no way has a single documentary market or culture emerged on a global scale. Indeed, as Sparks rightly observes, a cultural market unaffected by national forces and governed by "supra-state needs and values" alone is an academic myth, and an embattled one at that. In the case of television, "global" programs tend to be made by national producers, regulated by national policy makers, and watched by national audiences whose response is presumably dictated by local ways of seeing.[7] Most market studies support this conclusion, with one global survey concluding that two-thirds of the most popular shows in each market and in most genres are domestic in origin.[8] At the same time, recent analyses of international television suggest a continued attachment to domestic styles and topics.[9]

Documentary studies themselves suggest that television is more national than "global" in scope. Citing a 1996 report by Italy's RAI broadcasting group, for instance, both Kilborn[10] and Winston[11] have concluded that documentaries tend to survive (though not necessarily thrive) in areas with distinct public service broadcasting traditions. Even "global" programs—such as those carried by the Discovery network and other transnational specialty channels—tend to be far less popular than their local counterparts on regular terrestrial television (not including satellite or foreign cable channels). While this research has little to say about financing and distribution per se, it does suggest that documentaries are produced and consumed more or less domestically in every market we know about.

Again, market data tend to support these findings. To begin with, there is very little evidence to suggest that factual programmers think globally when it comes to scheduling or marketing. Indeed, very few take a chance on productions designed for worldly oriented audiences. Shows like Singapore STV 12's *World Journeys*, which encourages viewers to "explore and understand a myriad of cultures,"[12] or Finnish public broadcaster YLE's *World Television,* which "shows what life is like in another country,"[13] are certainly not the rule in domestic documentary schedules. Similarly, Europe's ARTE channel, which provides a reasonably multicultural lineup for European audiences, and America's Documentary Channel, which pledges to offer international programming for American viewers, seem to be quite exceptional on cable and satellite services. Most channels are not nearly so cosmopolitan. A study of Britain's major terrestrial services, for instance, has found that documentary programming concerning international topics actually fell by 40 percent in the early 1990s, illustrating a clear "trend towards insularity" in that market.[14] And while British factual programming about developing countries rose by 20 percent in 2001, according to the same studies, programs taking a "hard look" at local social issues seem to have been largely replaced by docusoaps and holiday "challenges."[15] Even in supposedly outward-looking markets, broadcasters such as TV New Zealand's Natural History Unit have pledged to buy fewer international documentaries in the wake of takeovers and cutbacks.[16] Ostensibly global broadcasters have taken a similarly isolationist line, with CNN reportedly purchasing less than one-fourth of its investigative reports from non-American sources in the late 1990s.[17]

And it may not just be the programmers who are parochial. Conventional wisdom suggests that domestic viewers prefer domestic documentaries as well, dictating supply through various channels of demand. Producers from around the world claim their audiences are interested in affairs close to home, though precise research in this area is inconclusive (since foreign shows are often promoted and scheduled with indifference).[18] At the same time, academics have noted the particular importance of domesticity in factual television, where programs lacking familiar time and space referents are apparently unpopular with most viewers.[19] Meanwhile, most programmers do everything they can to "relocate" imported programs by using previews and sometimes extra voice-overs to connect them with local content and embed them in domestic lineups.[20] All of this is intended to make global programs more local. Foreign documentaries are an example of this trend, as they are usually given a domestic context—a local music score, for instance, or a supporting commentary—to link the shows to affairs closer to home. While no comprehensive content analysis on this subject exists, the argument that global documentaries are essentially "redomesticized" by these devices and by the overall architecture of a lineup—by air times, advertisements, and surrounding programs—seems plausible enough as a description of documentary programming around the world. Producer Philip Hampson's observation that his portrait of the whales of Canada's Trinity Bay was "an entirely new experience" on Chinese television reminds us that local positionings as well as local preoccupations make documentary programming less international than it might appear.[21] Far from "going global," then, most documentary producers and distributors seem to be pitching domestic stories to domestic audiences—much as they did in documentary's national public service age.

Finally, documentary globalization may be impeded by factors more technical and political than cultural per se. In a digital convergence era, for instance, different standards of high-definition television transmission can discourage documentary program transfers, especially where profits are marginal.[22] Moreover, in a "free market" with fewer regulatory barriers, nations can and do impose restrictions on documentary program imports, even those for which an effective market exists.[23] Finally, national copyright idiosyncrasies may make documentary footage unaffordable or even inaccessible to foreign markets.[24] Of course, trade restrictions are not immutable, and they may be subject to a long-term erosion on all these fronts. Technically, program transfers may become increasingly affordable.[25] Legally, copyright restrictions may be overcome with the help of international organizations such as the Federation of Commercial and Audiovisual Libraries International.[26] And policy-wise, burdensome regulations may be eliminated as trading partners open their borders to cultural products. It is worth noting, for instance, that no signatory to World Trade Organization (WTO) agreements has opted out so that it can stop documentaries and other cultural imports as a national exception to free-trade clauses.[27] But even if technical, legal, and market forces continue to tilt toward a seamless world market, they hardly guarantee a free flow of documentary images, even in theory—that is, assuming there were a domestic market for these programs in the first place. Again, the idea of a cosmopolitan documentary seems to be just that—an idea rather than a reality with any grounding in existing markets or cultures.

What is most evident from a global review, then, is the stubborn parochialism of the documentary form—its persistence, for the most part, as a means of national self-expression by which grounded institutions represent their own places and issues in more or less culturally specific ways. In all these respects, a factual global monoculture seems a distant prospect indeed.

The Case for Documentary Globalization

Nonetheless, a plausible case for documentary globalization can be made—at least if we embrace the second definition of the term. That is, documentary can be seen as a "complexly connective" endeavor in which national public service institutions play a major role but in ways transformed and sometimes diminished by forces beyond their own borders. In this view, globalization and localization are not mutually exclusive; instead, they complement as well as contradict each other in shaping documentary practice.

There are many ways in which conventional critiques of globalization miss this big connective picture. Skeptical accounts, for instance, fail to account for the simultaneous importance of the global and the local in documentary production. To begin with, critics often overrate the significance of local public service institutions or regard them abstractly apart from their larger global environment. Certainly many public service broadcasting institutions are not as robust as the examples featured in documentary studies. Indeed most nations outside Europe, North America, and pockets of Asia lack a credible public sector altogether, and most are simply unable to produce regular audiovisual documents of themselves for audiences at home and abroad—a basic public service function if ever there were one. Not surprisingly, a very few European and North American countries dominate the international factual television market, and they alone are able to produce and export documentaries on a regular basis. One report suggests the United States controlled 37 percent of the factual market in 1996–1997 (the most recent years for which figures were available), with the United Kingdom following at 18 percent, Australia and Canada at 4 percent and 3 percent, respectively, and most other countries not even showing up on the scale.[28] Production is similarly skewed in the documentary sector, which most studies examine separately from "pop-doc" fare such as reality and current affairs programming. One study suggests that in 2000 Europe and North America together produced and acquired 57 percent of the 935,549 hours of documentary programming broadcast around the world and accounted for a full 75 percent of the US$400 million global market. Africa and the Middle East, by comparison, accounted for just 8 percent of the hours and 1 percent of the documentary market value, with most other regions falling somewhere in between (but in terms of market value toward the low end of the scale).[29] This is certainly not the only globally invisible market. Asian factual television exports, for instance, are almost nonexistent with the exception of those from Japan and often take the form of raw footage that is bartered rather than sold on the world market.[30]

But the tenuousness of factual self-expression is also evident in stronger documentary markets. That is, even nations with well-established public service traditions may be unable to provide compelling documentary images for themselves and other markets. Take France, for instance, sometimes described as an "impenetrable fortress" because of the protection it provides its own cultural market in a global era.[31] For all its cultural efforts, the French market still lacks the ability to produce "internationally-oriented projects of high quality," according to one leading independent producer.[32] In fact, in 1996–1997, that country controlled just 1 percent of the world trade in factual television.[33] Canada is another example of the precariousness of domestic documentary. America's northern neighbor has one of the highest levels of cultural support in the world, a fair amount of it directed toward domestic factual and documentary programming. Yet even here, foreign and particularly American documentary imports have made serious incursions. Recent research suggests that while 92 percent of Canadians who watch TV news turn to Canadian programs, just 36 percent of public affairs viewers do the same, a radical drop since 1984, when these programs captured nearly two-thirds of the domestic market.[34] While similar figures are unavailable in Australia, that country's Film Commission (AFC) has reported a "continuing downward pressure on the budgets of local [documentary] television programs" and, at least potentially, a corresponding inability to compete with foreign specialty channels for domestic viewers.[35] A joint report by the AFC and the Australian Film Finance Corporation (FFC) further indicates that country's domestic documentary sector has experienced little growth, with the value of production in 1997–1998 (the most recent years for which figures are available) falling to less than the average over the previous nine years. In short, Australia's ability to compete with documentary imports seems to have been severely undermined at all levels.[36] The Australian Broadcasting Authority further suggests that lower-budget shows remain "vulnerable to import replacement" by glossier foreign productions that are effectively dumped below cost on the domestic market.[37] Of course there is a place for high-quality domestic documentaries on Australian television. Local factual shows are priority programming for the Australian Broadcasting Corporation (ABC), for instance, which is also required by its charter to maintain editorial control over coproductions with foreign producers. However, even public service programs may be re-versioned for foreign markets, which is increasingly the case as independent producers aggressively pursue foreign financing and export markets to offset declining domestic budgets.[38] Even in strong public service cultures, then, documentary production is often decisively shaped, and sometimes undermined, by transnational forces.

Domestic markets face even starker challenges outside the Euro-American-Asian public service corridor. Again, there is little reliable information here regarding the relative audience shares for domestic and foreign documentary programming, but some evidence does suggest increased levels of foreign financing and foreign-directed content. For instance, Israel's New Foundation for Cinema and Television, which receives government support for independent documentaries, reports that producers frequently seek global financing in the form of pre-sales or coproductions because of a fragmented market and declining license fees.[39] At the same time, they seem to be focusing more on issues of interest to the transnational market per se. Domestically oriented programs are still shown on Israel's public channel, but documentary imports are gaining ground, especially on the commercial Channel 8, which buys more than 90 percent of its documentary programs from foreign sources.[40]

A global orientation is also evident in Asia, where traditionally closed markets are opening up to foreign capital. In some respects, China bucks the globalization trend, as its audiences have traditionally preferred local programs, making even coproductions mostly "unsuitable for the home viewer," according to one local programmer.[41] But this situation may be changing. Declining advertising revenues and currency evaluations that have helped keep program imports at bay also force local broadcasters to fill their schedules with cheap shows and repeats, making them less able to compete with foreign services when they appear. Discovery Networks International is taking advantage of this situation by selling blocks of nature shows to cable stations in more than thirty Chinese cities, dramatically widening its entry into the Chinese market, where satellite programming has hitherto been unaffordable or inaccessible to most viewers. Similar efforts are being made by the National Geographic Channel.[42] At the same time, declining domestic revenues are forcing local producers to give up homegrown filmmaking for globally marketable productions. Emerging new genres like wildlife shows and diaspora cultural portraits, for instance, generally receive 10 to 20 percent of their budgets from foreign sources and have become the lifeblood for local filmmakers who, like one Hong Kong independent, find they "cannot survive" on domestically oriented shows alone.[43]

Documentary markets are even more affected by globalization in Latin America, where production geared for a single home market is strictly limited. Local terrestrial and pay channels generally avoid documentaries altogether, conceding the market to foreigners while concentrating on *telenovela*-type programming and local news. Foreign satellite services like the Discovery Channel, on the other hand, avoid domestic acquisitions because of low ratings in the Latin American market, leaving domestic documentaries in limbo (though, as we shall see in the next chapter, the network has established a regional production workshop in Miami and promises more domestic programs in years to come). Mundo Olé, for its part, takes more than 60 percent of its documentaries from its parent A&E network and purchases most of the rest from outside Latin America.[44] Few local producers survive in these conditions, and those that do tend to favor transnationally oriented product. Filmmakers like Brazil's Fernando Grifa broaden stories "so that [they] interest other people."[45] Similarly, a growing number of "disastertainment" producers tailor their programs for foreign and regional syndication markets. Even taking into account these homegrown productions, fully 80 percent of the documentaries shown on Latin American television are foreign imports.[46]

A global survey thus reveals starkly varied capacities and influences in documentary markets around the world. But for all the differences, most nations do not retain a full-fledged documentary capacity that places them above and beyond the influence of transnational marketplaces. Such an assertion about their capacity is partly accurate with respect to wealthy American and European nations enjoying the benefits of a public service broadcasting tradition, but it is almost certainly misplaced elsewhere. To be sure, most of the world retains some potential for documentary self-expression, but this potential is increasingly shaped by forces beyond national borders.

Documentary "Glocalization"

But shaped in what way? As was suggested earlier, globalization can complement as well as contradict local documentary markets. Coproductions, for instance, can enable local documentary production, at least in the right circumstances. Indeed, a historical perspective suggests that even the purest public service forms came into being with the help of bilateral or multilateral cooperation. The first international coproduction, for instance, was a 1953 documentary collaboration between the BBC and the U.S. Educational and Television Service (the forerunner of PBS).[47] A later arrangement, known as "Intertel," provided for regularized program exchanges between the world's national public broadcasters in the 1960s and early 1970s (to encourage what was called a "wider understanding of world").[48] Film coproductions were developed on an official basis in the 1950s and 1960s, often between commonwealth nations or like-minded partners.[49] Exchanges of documentary magazine programs became more commonplace in the 1970s, when the "Intermag" treaty allowed members to purchase from an international pool of programs at cost, thereby defraying rising production expenses. And by the 1980s, most public service broadcasters had established their own international sales divisions with catalogues that often featured documentary programs.[50] Even in the most firmly entrenched public service cultures, documentary was conceived as something more than a national project.

Of course, none of this amounted to documentary globalization per se. In the public service sector, international exchanges essentially involved the organized transfer of programs between nation-states for cultural rather than commercial purposes.[51] Even within these limits, documentary exports were limited. Technically, for instance, some countries embraced 16 mm standards for documentary films and programs, which made exports difficult.[52] Divergent organizational cultures also emerged, with one producer at the Canadian Broadcasting Corporation (CBC) noting the "difficulty of selling [documentary] programs planned and produced to [our] parameters to the very different world of US and foreign television."[53] National priorities also differed. For example, Canadian producers were warned "not to put foreign audiences ahead of our own" and to keep in mind that the real "key to success" in documentary and current affairs programming was what "we [at the CBC] produced for ourselves."[54] Clearly, documentaries in the public service age were mostly regarded as a means by which the nation-state represented its own places to its own people.

But a less predictable global market for documentaries also emerged at this time, guided less by state cultural priorities. Curtin has noted the prominence of documentary programs in early global syndication markets; the American NBC network, for instance, exported its "special reports" to more than fifty countries in the early 1960s.[55] In the years that followed, independent producers and private broadcasters came to appreciate documentaries as market commodities in their own right, and an upsurge of market activity became apparent in the 1980s and even more so in the next decade. Transnationalization was in some respects required by weaker domestic environments. Government supports and domestic license fees—the key ingredients of a national broadcasting system—began to decline, forcing producers to seek funding beyond their borders. At the same time, a growing demand for documentaries was evident in the global marketplace as foreign investors found documentaries cheaper to produce, easier to sell, and simpler to show than other program types. The average budget for a one-hour program in 1998, for instance, was just Cdn$350,000, compared to Cdn$1.2 million for drama, according to one report from the global MIP-TV market.[56]

Investors also found documentaries profitable in the long term. Documentary programs, it turned out, could be rebroadcast, and they tended to enjoy a longer shelf life than news or current affairs shows. The shows often had a broader global appeal than their factual counterparts because their higher shooting rations yielded extra footage that could be reedited and repackaged for foreign versions. Already in the early 1980s, Canadian documentarists were speaking of the "changed realities of [documentary] television" that led them to keep an eye on international as well as domestic markets.[57] By the mid-1990s, 24.4 percent of international coproductions were documentaries, the second highest share after dramas.[58] By 2001, documentaries were reported to be the world's single most common type of coproduction.[59]

Of course, "globalized" or not, documentaries are still rightly associated with national finance markets. One recent worldwide survey actually suggests that 72 percent of documentary budgets are raised domestically and only 28 percent from international sources.[60] But at the same time, just one-fourth of documentary productions proceed with no foreign financing whatsoever.[61] And tellingly, producer polls suggest that only one-third of documentary producers consider international partnerships to be unimportant to their success.[62] Thus in production circles, documentary programming tends to be regarded as both a global and local endeavor.

The "glocal" nature of documentary can further be seen in corporate reports. In many parts of the world, for instance, foreign financing is seen as the only way to sustain production of any kind. Brazil's Giros Productions is a case in point, channeling the proceeds of its global work for Discovery Networks International and MTV Brazil into local cultural programs "from [a Brazilian] perspective and for [Brazilian] bene-fit."[63] In a similar way, Canada's Arnait Productions funds its aboriginal documentaries with the help of foreign cable reve-nues via the Canadian Television Fund. Not surprisingly, the International Documentary Association cites foreign financ-ing as a necessary component of almost any documentary pro-duction.[64] Even more culturally minded public service advo-cates recognize the importance of transnational projects. The European Broadcasting Union launched a coproduction group in 1996 that has developed fifty-seven documentary ventures between member and nonmember states. Group Chair Axel Arno notes that "only the BBC and the big German and French broadcasters can survive by doing big budget documentaries by themselves."[65] Taken together, market statistics and pro-ducer reports suggest that documentaries are best viewed as local projects whose condition of possibility is a transnational marketplace.

Global and local dimensions are also evident in documen-tary distribution. Rofekamp describes a "two-tier market" in which producers turn to conventional and specialty channels to get projects off the ground.[66] Neither tier, in his view, is self-sufficient, and most programs circulate between the two. Transnational specialty channels are clearly the growth sector, now accounting for 70 percent of the volume and 41 percent of the market value of documentaries worldwide.[67] Services such as these reach more territories more efficiently while offering shorter, non-exclusive deals that allow producers to sell pro-grams to more than one buyer. But transnational deals can be legal nightmares since signals can be received in more than one territory. They also require more service work, as pro-ducers must pay the costs for tapes, transport, licenses, and royalties. Most consultants thus advise producers to "strategize and maneuver" between national and transnational levels to make documentaries pay off.[68] Again, global and local chan-nels are best seen as distinct but increasingly codependent out-lets for documentary distribution.

All in all, then, production and distribution practices suggest that documentary has been globalized at least in a qualified sense. No country is able to factually represent itself independently of the global market, and this applies to both marginal players and documentary superpowers. Moreover, national and local players that continue to play a part in documentary production have themselves been helped, hindered, and decisively reshaped by forces beyond their own borders. These new spaces of production are perhaps best appreciated if we take a look at specific cases of "glocalization"—that is, at institutions operating on both global and local market levels.

Global Documentary Festivals

In the world of documentaries, complex connectivity is most evident in the case of film festivals. Gatherings of international productions and producers, for instance, have become a well-established documentary tradition, with more than 2,500 festivals taking place around the world.[69] Some festivals, such as South Africa's Encounters event, showcase distinctly local subjects and styles that are seen to represent particular cultures. Others, such as the Amsterdam International Documentary Film Festival, the Sheffield International Documentary Festival, and Marseilles' Sunny Side of the Doc, serve as venues for mostly "cultural" documentaries. Still others, including South Africa's Sithengi Film Festival and New York's Independent Film Project, are explicitly designed to build local connections to a global marketplace.

The world's largest documentary festivals, however, are frankly corporate in intent. Hong Kong's International Film and Television Market, for instance, brings together market players from across China and the rest of Asia. Toronto's Hot Docs festival claims to be the "largest gathering of international documentary financiers" in North America,[70] showing projects from more than eighty-eight countries in its 2000 lineup.[71] And MIPDOC, an offshoot of the MIP-TV market and perhaps the largest documentary festival in the world, brings together producers and programmers from more than fifty-three countries to meet "global documentary demand."[72] Some observers believe festivals are becoming more regional and re-trenching from the worldwide market to a certain extent, with national events such as the National Association of Television Program Executives (NATPE) annual conference of U.S. syndicators growing at the expense of transnational showcases like MIPDOC.[73] But as a worldwide phenomenon, festivals still bring together dispersed factual filmmakers, and in this sense they must be seen as global institutions.

But of what sort? Clearly not all festivals are created equal, and these gatherings can be seen as examples not just of complex connection but of a sort of documentary domination of large countries over small. More precisely, they may allow for the imposition of a dominant market style on producers around the globe. There is in fact some evidence that larger festivals—often of the regional or national variety—are eclipsing their smaller counterparts and with them perhaps local, less commercially oriented styles of filmmaking. The emergence of the Hong Kong International Film and Television Market as a dominant force in Asia, for instance, is perhaps evidence of a sort of consolidated commercialism occasioned by China's entry into the World Trade Organization (WTO). Centralization may also bring with it a degree of cultural homogenization as China begins to approach factual filmmaking as a potential export in which a regional corporate style is preferred.[74] The worldwide spread of festival "pitching" sessions—where independent projects are assessed and sometimes purchased by network commissioning editors—is just one example of a loosely defined "market standard" being established and enforced around the world.

But corporate hegemony hardly results in a full-fledged documentary monoculture and the eclipse of the local that goes with it. To begin with, smaller festivals and local independent styles will almost certainly survive in the wake of festival and market consolidation. Indeed, one might argue that independent venues complement the corporate filmmaking world by developing talent and products that can be "leveraged" into mass markets (a point I will address more fully in chapter 4). Further, not all festivals complement larger markets in a straightforward fashion. Some festivals eschew the "documart" format, while others deliberately cultivate local, uncommercial styles. Festivals like Australia's REAL: Life on Film gathering are explicitly designed as counterweights to the global market, encouraging producers to cultivate local styles and "tackle new themes" in their work.[75] India's Mumbai International Film Festival similarly stresses indigenous works from around the world. Meanwhile, the European Documentary Network's European Storytellers event promotes itself as a "pitching free zone" where the focus is on "ethics and the aesthetics of today's documentary film."[76]

Even if we dismiss these efforts as holdouts or mere capitalist anomalies, a strict distinction between the "local" and the "global" and the "alternative" and the "mainstream" in documentary production is hard to sustain. The growing presence of independent producers at major market festivals belies such a dichotomy—with the roster of independent films dramatically increasing at gatherings such as Hot Docs just as a corporate presence seems to have declined.[77] While it would be wrong to say that festivals allow for a free diffusion of factual filmmaking styles, they hardly impose (European or American) market principles on the rest of the world in a straightforward way.

Finally, aside from allowing at least a degree of documentary diversity, festivals enable the movement of technologies, ideas, monies, and personnel across borders, which may in turn give rise to something more than straight documentary uniformity. Festivals often allow for the pooling of production resources, as is the case with New York's Kick Start event, which allows independents from around the world to share footage and equipment. They may provide for physical or virtual gatherings of documentary producers, as is the case in the world's first documentary cyberfestival, D-film (the Website of which claims to let "people go places they could never go").[78]

They may facilitate the movement of capital across borders, allowing producers to "cook deals in one country and close deals in another," as one Hot Docs organizer puts it.[79] And finally, they may encourage new forms of global reflexivity, leading filmmakers to reassess and reshape their activities in light of documentary practice elsewhere.

This last aspect is perhaps the hardest to assess, but it can be seen at a number of levels of production. Reflexivity may take the form of self-styled "cosmopolitanism," as in the case of the Australian International Documentary Conference, which is designed to overcome that country's "isolation" from the "style, the discussion and the views of the international community."[80] It can be seen in a more globally attuned market savvy of the sort claimed by the Australian Film Commission, which tracks the market success of Australian international festival entries to guide its own domestic funding decisions. It may entail a degree of self-examination, like the "public consciousness of documentary's importance" that the International Documentary Association says results from its various screening events.[81] Or it may result in a full-blown critical awareness: either on the part of viewers who may develop a "concern for solidarity and world affairs," as Amnesty International puts it, or on the part of producers who may engage in "vigorous debates about ideas, treatments, style and innovation," according to South Africa's INPUT festival.[82] In these more or less global spaces we see a degree of mutual awareness and interaction between hitherto separate documentary monies. It is here, beyond the confines of the nation-state, that many new varieties of documentary practice evolve. Indeed, this sort of global space seems to be emerging in another ubiquitous documentary institution: the actuality format.

Global Documentary Formats

Formats, like festivals, illustrate the simultaneously global and local nature of documentary production today. Formats essentially consist of program plans—such as docusoap and reality concepts—that are produced, promoted, and tested in multiple markets. As such, they serve as vehicles for the circulation of ideas and thus the globalization of documentary as a mode of factual presentation. Fundamentally, formats tend to reduce the costs and boost the benefits of documentary exports. They yield lucrative global revenues, earning export owners an average 5 percent royalty fee for each series. And they help settle thorny rights disputes, allowing parties to settle their differences through the newly created Format Recognition and Property Association. Formats thus make documentaries easier to develop and defend as global properties.[83]

At the same time, documentary formats can be seen to enable domestic production by minimizing the resources needed for program development. For local programmers, they are generally cheap and profitable: less risky than homegrown story ideas and more adaptable than straight program acquisitions. They also tend to cost much less than either type, offering global economies of scale in customized packages.

Reality shows—particularly cop programs and docusoaps—are the best-known documentary format, and they illustrate the current reach and limits of factual ideas on a worldwide scale. The shows themselves seem to be somewhat international in origin. By some accounts, reality programs started out in the United States, their roots in the "true detective" radio shows of the 1930s and the TV crime dramas of the 1950s and 1960s.[84] Other studies trace the genre back to Europe and the early crime-watcher series on German television that combined documentary footage with dramatic inserts and live action.[85] Whatever their origins, there are now more than 900 reality shows around the world, according to a recent New on the Air (NOTA) survey.[86] The *Big Brother* format alone was sold to sixteen countries by Endemol as of May 2001 and was a hit in every one except the United States.[87] The major U.S. networks, for their part, offered twenty of their own reality shows in the fall of 2001, making the reality format a full-fledged worldwide hit.

But in what sense do reality formats continue to be local? In academic and legal circles, the shows generally are dismissed as copycats that allow producers to duplicate or steal each other's projects instead of generating homegrown ideas. Dovey has described reality shows as a "strange exotic variety" that threatens to eclipse local documentary traditions.[88] Meanwhile, court systems have generally had a hard time distinguishing between competing local formats and determining where global formula begins and genuine local spin leaves off. A five-year dispute between Britain's Castaway Productions and the Dutch Endemol group over rights to the *Survivor* format, for instance, suggests that even legal experts have had a hard time telling one documentary idea from another.[89]

Format productions similarly suggest that documentary differences are more fiction than fact. U.K.-based program distributor Action Time, for instance, offers clients what it calls a documentary "bible"—an "incredibly comprehensive guide" explaining how the show has been produced in a primary market and how it should be produced in another. Possible variations are carefully reviewed before formats go into production.[90] Meanwhile, the world's most successful format producer, Endemol, insists on "full consultancy" based on a "bible," a complete set of tapes and a team of advisors to make sure, as a director of sales notes, that "things are produced the way we think they should be."[91] In the case of *Big Brother*, the firm only allows for minor local adjustments to set designs and crews. Formatters may also leave their mark by insisting on "block sales" by which local buyers are provided with new shows every year whether they want them or not. In cases like these, local markets may give up any semblance of creative control. Indeed, "creativity," such as it is, tends to be the province of a small team of globe-trotting reality producers who, by some accounts, impose their Endemol-type visions on local markets, dictating popular documentary styles around the world.[92] In these cases, "cultural connection" may amount to nothing more than a simple leveling out (and dumbing down) of the documentary form.

But local resistance is also evident. First, differences between documentary formats have survived in a variety of countries, at least in legal terms. Denmark, for instance, has enacted specific unfair competition laws to prevent clonings of shows, and if other countries follow suit, producers may be encouraged to develop their own homegrown products to avoid litigation.[93] At the same time, producers seem to be trying to make programs distinct in fact as well as in case law. Most format holders take a more hands-off approach to their franchises than does Endemol; the owner of the Australian *Popstars* format provides buyers with a concept statement, some background market research, and not much else. Foreign blueprints and foreign crews are not part of these packages.[94]

A format is thus best regarded as a mobile apparatus for the production of more or less local television content. While formats as an institution suggest that documentaries are less and less removed from forces beyond their home markets, they also remind us that production is rarely carried out according to a distant formula—even in the clone-friendly world of infotainment television.

Conclusion

Globalization has hardly eroded national documentary institutions. Various forms of factual self-expression survive and even thrive in today's transnational television marketplace. But these facts hardly call documentary globalization into question. Indeed, globalization is not a zero-sum process that proceeds at the expense of national or local culture. As we have seen in the case of formats and festivals, more or less local documentaries are often produced by the forces of global capital. At the same time, capital cycles do not exist in virtual space alone and are anchored in what Saskia Sassen has called "territorial frontier zones"[95]—grounded spaces for the local production and consumption of culture. In this sense at least, globalization and localization are complementary processes.

But the question remains: What sorts of programs and texts will we see in an era of documentary globalization? That is, how will documentaries represent particular people and places in a more or less connected world? It is this fundamental question—this first global dimension of documentary—that I want to consider in the next chapter.

THREE

Global Documentary and Place

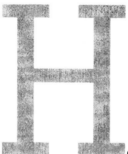ow will places be represented
in global documentaries? Will they be portrayed as bordered
locations in a more connected world? Will they be documented
in culturally unique ways? And will they stand out as distinct
entities in a global marketplace of signs? These are important
questions for our understanding of documentary, television,
and culture in general. After all, both public broadcasting systems and their defining genres tend to be judged for their
representation of citizen-viewers in the actual conditions in
which they live. In some respects, documentaries, documentary media, and documentary cultures stand or fall on their
representations of place.

In this chapter I want to examine a number of institutions
that seem to challenge documentary representation as such.
In the first part of the chapter, I will focus on coproductions,
formats, and factual superchannels. In the second, I will examine modes of representation that act as a sort of local counter-
weight to these forces. And in my conclusion, I will consider
the status of locales in emerging documentary forms.

Place as an Object of Representation

But before we tackle these issues, we should consider a basic preliminary question. That is: What exactly is a documentary "place"? How are we to understand place as a disputed object of representation around the world? And how should we expect places to be represented in the documentary texts of the future?

We should be wary of generalizations, for as we shall see there are many popular ways of answering these questions. But in policy discourses, at least, places tend to be regarded as fixed objects of documentary representation—that is, as intrinsically meaningful sites that are more or less available for faithful audiovisual recording. In Australian policy documents, for instance, documentary is expected to "reflect a sense of [national] identity, character and cultural diversity," thereby contributing to the goals of local content legislation as interpreted by the Australian Film Finance Corporation and the Australian Film Commission.[1] In the *Pacific Islanders in Communications* guidelines issued by the American PBS network, documentaries should "illuminate [local] experience" and foster a "deeper understanding of values inherent in Pacific Island cultures."[2] And in the guidelines for the Canadian Television Fund, publicly supported documentaries should be "visibly Canadian," dealing with actual Canadian people, issues, events, achievements and locales."[3]

Even globally oriented institutions tend to accord place a special primordial status. In international public broadcasting culture, as interpreted by the annual International Public Television (INPUT) conference, "documentaries should truly represent their own cultures."[4] And in New Zealand's more export-centered broadcast guidelines, documentaries should offer "significant [domestic] content or address local concerns."[5] At the very least, authorities around the world pay lip service to the local as an object of representation that somehow dictates its own style.

Of course, place-based content and style can be hard to define in precise terms. The Irish Film Board, for instance, favors "genuine Irish film making" over commercial export projects but offers few guidelines concerning what such an approach might entail.[6] Similarly, the Australian Broadcasting Authority defines local documentary as "programming for the cultural benefit of Australians" that also "contributes to the development of a local production industry," but it offers few specifics beyond that.[7] Meanwhile, that country's Film Finance Corporation supports "local" films concerned with international subjects "which may not be attractive to foreign investors"— with little further specification.[8]

Definitions of the local can also be as impractical as they are vague. In most countries, local documentaries need not deal with local places at all, at least in any obvious way. In Canada, for instance, independent producers have persuaded the government that films set and shot outside of Canada should receive support as local productions from the Canadian Television Fund and the Canadian Radio-television and Telecommunications Commission.[9] Meanwhile at the provincial level, local filmmakers successfully lobbied British Columbia regulators to waive a 1998 tax requirement that at least 75 percent of spending and principal photography take place within provincial boundaries, arguing that they had to "go all over the world to film a story."[10] Finally, the Canadian Independent Film Caucus has persuaded the Canadian Television Fund that local documentaries should be defined not by their subject matter but by their style, which is "less sensationalistic, more complex and more considered than American television fare."[11] In Canada, then, local content quotas have proved to be either burdensome or banal: unduly restrictive, or largely incapable of guiding funding decisions in the first place. With policy waffling like this, it is easy to see why cultural sovereigntists fear that place will survive as offshore production base but not much else in the documentary networks of the future.

Notwithstanding these ambiguities, regulators continue to insist that documentaries "reflect" or at least define something

local. At times, documentaries are seen to require some sort
of local subject to merit support. At others, local subjects are
seen to require some form of documentation to exist in the first
place. Paradoxically, perhaps, documentary places are seen to
be not just fixed and foundational but contingent: requiring a
steady stream of authentic self-images to keep identity both in
mind and "in place," so to speak. According to the industry-
based Australian Documentary Foundation, for instance, local
documentaries are the nation's indispensable "vehicles of record," reminding citizens of their "distinct character."[12] And according to the PBS-based *Pacific Islanders in Communications*
guidelines, documentaries are the world's "compass points,"
underscoring a "resonance of indigenous issues and concerns
in a changing world."[13] The link between documentation and
cultural identity is thus commonplace in cultural discourse.
For producer Martyn Burke, the documentary cultural impera-
tive is clear-cut: "Are we going to do anything Canadian [in
documentary programming]," he asks, "or is Canada going to
be this Nowhere land?"[14] In this view there can be no meaningful documentaries without a local or national referent.

And equally certainly, there can be no local or national referent without audiovisual support—no nation, that is, without
documentary representation.

Global Challenges to Local Documentary

Viewed this way, documentary places are clearly under threat
in a global marketplace. That is, regarded as fixed but fragile
sites—as unique locales in need of a documentary spotlight—
places face a number of challenges in the new political economy of factual television.

First and foremost, perhaps, local documentary traditions
are seen to be compromised by placeless production: by the
making of programs in more than one locality, by more than
one producer for more than one market. Documentaries, as
we have seen, are the world's most frequently coproduced

type of program, and though this mode of production seems to have tapered off in recent years, frequently so has the amount of domestic financing involved—presumably resulting in less "local control" over a final product (see chapter 2). More than any other documentary practice, coproduction is seen to compromise genuine representation by and for cultures being represented.

The mechanics of homogenization—that is, the process by which coproductions cease to reflect particular places and culturally specific "ways of seeing"—vary in different accounts. According to Martyn Burke, coproduced local portraits are essentially watered down: "If you go to New York and say we've got this great idea and it involves Kenora, Ontario," he explains, "they're going to look at you blankly and say, 'If you can add Peoria as well as Kenora then we'll be happy.'"[15] By other accounts, coproductions are cliché: an official at Australia's Film Finance Corporation says export-oriented programs focus on "aborigines, sharks, remote tropical islands and red deserts."[16] And in other versions, coproductions eliminate the local entirely. Foreign financing results in foreign programs, according to producer John Kastner: "What we're starting to see [in Canada]," he notes, "is a new generation of filmmakers doing things like 'The Plague Monkeys' [a 1996 Canadian coproduction concerning the West African ebola plague] as opposed to Canadian stories because they're easier to get made and easier to sell."[17] In each case, critics believe local content is precluded by global financing. An official of Film Australia insists that the documentaries that are "harder to sell around the world are ones that look at contemporary life . . . where context is important, and each country would want to make their own."[18]

Global flows are also seen to stifle local documentary styles. Critics have noted a certain "cross-pollination" in nature documentaries[19] and the spread of a "British natural history" approach in markets as far afield as Australia, New Zealand, and Japan.[20] Producer Michael Kott notes similar trends in history programming that ends up as "homogenous mush" because of the demands of "different task masters."[21] Other critics point to the rise of "McDocumentaries" that avoid culturally specific references so they can be sold in markets across the world. McDocumentaries may engage the local generically, within "preset story forms," as producer Michael Kott puts it.[22] Or they may engage it casually at best, drawing upon assembly line production schedules to "fill program slots half a world away," as one critic claims.[23] In each case, however, locations "keep changing" while stories "remain curiously the same."[24]

From an academic point of view, many of these arguments are problematic. Critics often evoke an idealized pre-global moment in which transparent representation without mediation is possible—a moment when cultures exist "unstaged" and thus uncorrupted by global representation itself. But if we put aside the obvious essentialism, a good case can be made that global production practices preclude even a provisionally or contingently accurate representation of place. In today's marketplace, it is hard to imagine even "films of a community having a film made about itself."[25] Current production schedules rarely allow for sustained engagements with particular ways of life, however we conceive of them. As one freelance producer for Discovery Networks Europe observes, "When you have 6 shooting days and 2 to 3 weeks to edit you can't afford to just squirt out tape."[26] By other accounts as well, spending more than a week in a target location is a rarity in today's production market.[27]

Even "self-representation" may fail to address community concerns in a global factual age. Documentary portraits of local everyday life—particularly of the docusoap variety—sometimes adhere to narrative and visual plans designed half a world away, occasionally under the strict supervision of foreign film crews (as we saw in chapter 2). Documentary formats are cheaper and easier to produce than original domestic productions, but they may be only loosely grounded or connected to the places ostensibly producing them—the local franchise client. In some cases, franchised locales are actually reconstructed to meet the needs of a global production and not vice versa: Endemol, for instance, demands that its *Big Brother* reality sets be virtually identical in size and design around the world to protect its brand image.[28] In other cases, place may survive as a mere insert between program segments, with the Canada's Global Television Network promoting its airing of the *Survivor* series as a Canadian version because of a brief commentary by an ex-patriate former contestant. In these situations, the local leaves only the faintest of documentary traces—as a convenient program backdrop but not much else.

Even if documentary formats are fully "adapted" to local markets—drawing upon domestic concepts and talent—their overall design may preclude a sustained engagement with an identifiable culture. Docusoaps around the world, for instance, generally adhere to a "first-person" story structure that makes a discussion of collective issues and shared concerns a rarity.[29] Derek Paget has noted a similar trend in American and European docudramas that "focus on specific stories—often of private individuals projected by some experience or other into the public domain."[30]

As yet, policy makers have proven themselves unable or unwilling to "re-localize" documentaries in the face of these trends. The European Community's Eurodoc project, for instance, seeks to "protect the [local] works" of its member states "without reformatting them,"[31] but this initiative is generally seen to have floundered because of insufficient funds and excess red tape. Some critics even wonder if local factual production is amenable to any sort of state support in today's world markets. UNESCO's in-progress Convention on Cultural Diversity may well be trumped by various World Trade Organization and bilateral agreements, as have other cultural exemption clauses. Meanwhile, public funding supports already in place may be "too little, too late or too complicated," a Canadian producer says, to keep up with market developments.[32] More often than not, public officials seem unable to give local documentaries roots in the wake of global "deterritorialization" trends.

In short, critics are right to note a number of tensions between "embedded" representation and the largely disembedded
financial and conceptual flows of documentary production today. Coproductions and formats may not rule out self-docu-
mentation, but they certainly make it more problematic, and
it is at least conceivable that places—as they have been conceived in documentary discourse for nearly a century—will
either disappear or else survive as weightless signifiers in an
empty global mediascape—a mediascape that represents everywhere in general but nowhere in particular.

Global Supports for Local Documentary

Of course, for market advocates there are just as many reasons to believe that places will continue to be represented in
a documentary sense. Indeed, a closer look at contemporary
documentary institutions suggests that markets will provide
at least a minimal space for place, with or without regulatory
supports.

Coproductions can be seen to enable as well as constrain
local production. According to some critics, the pooling of
domestic and foreign finances is best regarded as a contract
(though not necessarily a symmetrical one) between local producers and global programmers—and can be negotiated to the
benefit of both. Canadian production companies, for instance,
often gain editorial control over their programs by seeking
only final chunks of funding outside Canada, once tax credits,
government funds, and domestic broadcast windows have been
secured; in other words, they approach the global market from
what they call "position of strength."[33] For similar reasons,
many producers seek only like-minded partners; Toronto's Associated Producers entered a recent permanent coproduction
deal with Britain's Channel 4 that apparently involves no sur-
render of local editorial control. Of course, smaller producers
may not have the clout to defend their interests this way. But
even if we do not take these categorical claims of cultural sov-

ereignty at face value, the straightforward equation of global financing with placeless content may be too simplistic.

Neither is it true, in an axiomatic sort of way, that factual formats preclude local representation of any sort. Suggestions that global reality formulas are running riot over local documentary styles—most evident in Jon Dovey's characterization of the docusoap as a sort of "exotic variety" threatening to gobble up other forms of documentary practice entirely—are certainly open to question.[34]

First, such a view tends to underestimate the degree to which even the most virulent of global strains—including reality imports—tend to be reshaped and hence "re-embedded" to some degree in home territories. Take the Canadian History Television channel's version of *Survivor*, for instance, which involves a "one-year experiment in Canadian pioneer living" portrayed in a "leisurely, respectful and cooperative" way "undreamed of by American Survivors," as one Canadian critic put it.[35] Unlike its American counterparts, *Pioneer Quest* offers few obvious payoffs, with the $100,000 reward money leaving winners with an estimated Cdn$3 an hour wage for their time; all the Canadian contestants get is a degree of privacy notably lacking on the *Big Brother* and *Survivor* sets. All of these features make for a program that incorporates the *Survivor* format within the essentially high cultural framework of Canadian public service broadcasting. *Pioneer Quest* fundamentally reworks the very terms and production relations of the American show and arguably recuperates it as a domestic text.

Beyond that, the production may help articulate a notion of the domestic in the first place. As the local reviews suggest, *Pioneer Quest* serves as an occasion to note (and celebrate) the essential differences between domestic and foreign television, thereby defining local documentary culture for viewers (or at least critics) at large. To dismiss the show as a mono-market offshoot or a documentary dumbing down is shortsighted in all these respects.

Instances of outright resistance to imported documentary formats further call into question a number of cultural nation-

alist critiques. In much of the world, for instance, the circulation of documentary formats has resulted not in local factual
traditions being steamrolled but in outright "culture wars"—
in struggles over the very styles and spaces to be included in
global and local representation. Protests over the *Loft Story*
series and its American-style intrusions into French private
life are just one case in point. There have been similar back-
lashes in Portugal and Greece since 2001, all directed at the
surveillance practices associated with global reality television.
These cases suggest formats are best regarded as flexible or
"embeddable" documentary practices, capable of yielding culturally specific portraits of people and places around the world.
Again, the simple equation of documentary border crossing
with cultural homogeneity seems simplistic at best.

Not only have cultural critics underestimated local counter-
efforts in many documentary home markets; they also may
have exaggerated the global intentions of transnational programmers themselves. In fact, other than the more aggressive international reality formatters, few industry players actually seek or serve a single worldwide mass market. This is
the case for the world's best-known documentary imperialist
—Discovery Networks International (DNI), the largest documentary producer on earth, responsible for about 20 percent
of output worldwide and reaching more than 1.2 billion people
in 147 countries.[36] Founded and based in Bethesda, Maryland,
DNI boasts of its influence in documentary markets around
the world. One executive says with only a touch of hyperbole,
"There is not a documentary maker on the planet who has not
been affected by Discovery . . . and we will play a role in all
narrative and technological advances in the form."[37]

This impact notwithstanding, Discovery hardly imposes a
single corporate style on its various target markets. In fact, the
corporation seems to be actively working against the development of a single factual television market of its own or anyone
else's making. In fact, a peculiar sort of documentary diversity—including place-based diversity—seems to lie at the heart
of Discovery's global investment strategy. Like most specialty

services, DNI officials believe there is more money to be made from customized services than from a standardized portfolio per se. Profits thus depend on some sort of product diversification. At times, this is seen to involve representing viewers in a traditional sense: the network's former senior vice-president, Chris Haws, notes that "most markets demand to see themselves reflected, and we are in the business of providing them with that service."[38] At other times diversification involves reshaping local demand and the active regional resegmentation of the audience, as Haws notes: "We also have to give the audience what they never knew they wanted."[39] But whether local differences are to be served or "discovered," they are the basis of DNI's global investment strategy, which essentially involves a multiplication of markets and thus further opportunities for capital accumulation. The world according to Discovery is not a mass market at all but a series of intersecting home territories and enclaves, all of which must be represented, and sometimes reshaped, so the corporation can make a robust overall profit. In this sense, diversification means the corporation must "connect" with audiences "where they are," as founder and CEO John Hendricks puts it, wherever that may be. To be successful, he says, "we need our service in India, for example, to be thought of as emanating from there."[40]

Of course the "there" to which Hendricks refers need not be a specific geographic site. In fact, DNI's conception of the "local" sometimes disregards place altogether. DNI's specialty services, for instance, often address audiences as taste communities rather than as local inhabitants. Discovery Networks Europe, according to managing director Joyce Taylor, must be "there" if people are "in the mood for travelling, technology, gardening, whatever,"[41] the "there" in this case being an affective domain—a state of mind rather than a physical locale. Indeed, because of political and cultural differences, "there isn't actually a place called Europe at all," Taylor says, and the network is better off pursuing a conventional specialty programming strategy in regions like this.[42] Even Discovery's complementary web network, which it claims is more locally based than television, is designed to meet largely deterritorialized "needs whether they be in health, travel, do-it-yourself or entertainment."[43]

Nonetheless, the bulk of DNI programming is grounded—and in a sense relocated—in specific territories. The Discovery Channel, Animal Planet, The Learning Channel, Discovery Health, Science, and Travel and Kids rarely appear as standardized services for global taste markets. Each is uplinked by regional headquarters in London, Miami, New Delhi, and Singapore and then repackaged and rescheduled for specific (usually national) areas. Programs themselves are often customized or "versioned" for each site. In less "mature" markets, customization may simply involve redubbing, subtitling, or minor adjustments. Until recently, for instance, Discovery's Japanese services only offered foreign programs with subtitles. India, Korea, Taiwan, and China received dubbed series, while Latin America was sent generic fare with limited local "on-air promotions."[44] But more extensive customization has taken place once these areas have matured—that is, once 70 percent of investment costs have been recouped (which can take three to five years).[45] Domestic services of this type generally offer programs that contain at least local commentary and segment inserts. Programs for Discovery Kids, for instance, usually follow a standard story structure but include original segments and story guides to give the lineup a local feel; simple dubbing is almost always avoided, though this would be the simplest way to enter a new market. A program official notes that "if it doesn't feel like it could be kids from that country doing that show, the show doesn't do well in that country."[46]

Flexible global strategies also guide Discovery's various regional production workshops. DNI's "first-time filmmakers" initiatives, for instance, seek both "universally themed projects" and programs offering insights into "local everyday life in the new millennium."[47] The search for transnational themes may place all sorts of limits on filmmaking as such. A Discovery Europe executive depicts the company's independent producers workshops as an environment where "you can see [the filmmakers] . . . trying to appeal to a Discovery style of film making . . . there are no pitches for typical auteur films that have their place in a European [documentary] tradition."[48] Self-censorship may not just be widespread but endemic in these cases. Even if it is not, the network itself may filter out culturally specific styles in favor of "local" projects that fit every one of its territories. Indeed, this worldwide strategy may account for the coproduction problems DNI has encountered with territories like France that have what it calls "a way of telling a story . . . so different from the rest of the world."[49]

But if "parochial" programs have little place in the Discovery lineup, embedded representations may be welcome. The Discovery Campus Masterschool guidelines for local filmmakers advise that "a local story . . . can be very powerful for viewers around the world" and can focus on either "unique experiences or basic human emotions." In this view, Discovery is a sort of coordinated local production network: a regionally diverse project that breathes new life into scattered initiatives by providing the "necessary knowledge and contacts for future work on the international level."[50] Clearly, DNI may override traditional notions of place in these projects. But in doing so, it claims to offer a sustainable model of local representation in a global age.

Regular operations at Discovery can also be seen to offer a transnational base for local programming. It is true that most Discovery shows are centrally purchased or developed in Bethesda or London, or else reviewed by regional headquarters. DNI's Business Affairs Unit vets most local ideas from the start or takes them on itself, while productions and program purchases are generally planned and negotiated on behalf of local "partners."[51] But a certain amount of "on-the-spot" commissioning and acquisition does take place, and local channels have been allotted more substantial budgets in recent years for program development (though the network will not say exactly how much). DNI further insists that global economies of scale "enable" local service by building local audiences, with Discovery's one-stop shopping network, for instance, allowing individual units to offer "real world information" about local ways of life along with the "greatest number of [global] programs" at an affordable price. DNI President Don Wear acknowledges that his network may "never be as local as [domestic services] Doordarshan in India or TV Globo in Brazil," but it has the added benefit "of offering a window on the world."[52]

Thus, DNI portrays itself as a global network that can effectively represent anywhere on earth. "If there ever was a global channel capable of being customized for each of its key target markets," claims a company official, "Discovery is it."[53] Customization and reterritorialization also seem to be trends at other documentary superchannels, though there are exceptions. At the American-centric (U.S.) History Channel, for instance, local service involves a single American lineup. However, very few global channels entirely disregard the local this way, by offering just one type of program about one type of place for one type of audience. France's Odyssey network builds itself around autonomous and mostly self-sufficient production and programming units that cater to particular markets. Similarly, though on a much more modest scale, the National Geographic Channel has established local "program enterprise groups" of independent producers.[54] In most cases, then, a strategy of "rationalized diversity" has been pursued that allows superchannels to cope with a varied cultural environment in the most cost-effective way. Again DNI is typical in this respect as it looks for a "range of programs and styles" concerning a "variety of subjects and places" around the world with "as much crossover and spin-off potential as possible."[55] Corporate diversity as such minimizes risks by drawing upon flexible labor markets and varied program portfolios, making sure "just the right mix of producer and product" is employed in any given circumstance.[56] At the same time, diversity as such maximizes profits by allowing the network to sell or leverage products in as many markets as possible.

In short, the new political economy of factual television can be seen as neither global nor local in a traditional sense. Services like DNI make programs "for the world and for your neighborhood," and as long as we accept the network's definitions of its key geographic terms, this assertion is well founded.[57] An analysis of global documentary production and distribution patterns thus seems to bear out not the cultural nationalist nightmare of placelessness but the somewhat more complex scenario of "glocalization" in which transnational networks "paradoxically produce more and more locally produced and consumed goods."[58]

Rethinking Place in a Global Documentary Age

But of course the question remains: What are these local "places" that global producers and distributors seem so keen to represent? Critics like Martyn Burke may be wrong about places disappearing or only surviving as generic traces on global television screens but still right to insist that effective local representation—and with it local identity—is jeopardized in a global marketplace. There is in fact a good deal of evidence to suggest that place, whatever its current status in particular genres or markets, has assumed an altogether more precarious position in global documentaries than it did in the age of public service. Take "Canada" as represented in the (1997) CTV four-part miniseries *The Bay*, which under the direction of a Toronto-based entertainment lawyer recast the history of the Hudson's Bay Company as an international story set in Montreal, Winnipeg, the Orkney Islands, and London, England. Or Ontario in John Kastner's (1997) *Hunting Bobby Oatway*, which under pressure from prospective American investors was almost eliminated even as a story backdrop to make way for a human-interest crime feature about a child molester (until Kastner took the film to the CBC and remade it as an analysis of the provincial justice system). In these cases, Canada serves as a functional and peripheral space in a global text, but it hardly remains a place to be represented for its own sake.

There are many similar examples. In nature, sports, and

entertainment documentaries, Canada often appears as a commodity sign used to promote a variety of goods and services—in the case of Real Action Pictures Extreme Sports a line of outdoor gear ("shown to very good advantage in the Rockies," according to CEO Angrove),[59] and in Marco and Mauro LaVilla's (1998) *Hang the DJ*, an array of clothing accessories, soundtracks, and even world-touring rave events, all with a "Canadian vibe."[60] In the promotional literature of the Bureau du film du Quebec and the Saskatchewan Film and Video Development Corporation, on the other hand, Canada itself emerges as a sort of simulacrum, filling in for (mythic) places around the world—offering international documentary location scouts everything from a "touch of Europe" in the case of Quebec to Saskatchewan's "five distinct climatic zones ranging from arctic to semiarid desert."[61] In such cases, "place" seems to have neither disappeared nor survived as a fixed signifier with stable meanings. Rather it has reemerged, as Jody Berland has put it in another context, as a "dispensable token susceptible to the requirements of commercial exchange."[62] In short, if cultural nationalist theories of "placelessness" remain unsubstantiated and largely implausible, so do market models suggesting a straightforward representation of locality in a global age.

Places in Programs: Discovery's *Africa*

Arguments about local representation are, of course, mostly speculative. That is, very few market critics or advocates offer much in the way of textual analysis to back up their various cultural claims. Systematic content analysis and in-depth semiotic research that might shed light on the way places are actually represented in a global age are notably lacking, as both sides essentially deduce their arguments about local representation from what we know about cultural production and distribution patterns. Here I want to offer a preliminary, but I hope suggestive, study of a global market program that documents a particular locale for a more or less transnational audience. This program I think gives us at least a cursory idea of the ways locality is represented, reworked, and, in a rationalized way, recuperated for a global image market.

Discovery Canada's *Africa* is just such a project. The special two-hour program was designed as a portrait of "sustainable conservation" efforts and local response in the southern part of the continent. The series was produced by Discovery Canada, which is 20 percent owned by the American Discovery Network (with remaining shares controlled by Canadian broadcasters and cable companies), and aired for broadcast in Canada and foreign markets in September 2001.[63]

Africa begins with an image of Kenya's rift valley, which, it becomes clear, is the show's home base. "This valley has taught us more about ancestors than just about any other place in the world," announces host Jay Ingram. "And this country, this continent is home to a staggering number of animals." He explains, "Over the next two hours, we will examine the sometimes strained relationship between Africa and its animals." Ingram then introduces a montage of shots from *Africa*'s story settings: a Tanzanian chimpanzee reserve, the desert mountains of northern Kenya, an elephant reserve in South Africa, and a butterfly "farm" on Kenya's west coast.

What links all these sites, explains the host, and what makes them of interest to the show is their wildlife, which is "one of Africa's great tourist charms but also a devastating problem for Africa's farmers." A biologist in Kenya testifies that only selective trapping can save lions from wholesale slaughter by local landowners. Further north, in Kenya's M'Pala reserve, a group of biologists works to "resolve the tension between preserving wildlife and continuing to develop the economies of the country," while colleagues attempt to "shed light on species and biodiversity." Meanwhile in Tanzania, Jane Goodall transforms what "40 years ago [was] a fairly desolate place" into a "work that has been called one of the world's greatest achievements." An interview with Goodall in Dar es Salaam, far away from what she calls her "timeless peace in the forest," is followed by a profile of Kenya's Koobi Fora game area and the Arabuko Soboke forest reserve on the east African coast, where "similar efforts to promote peaceful coexistence between people and animals are being made." *Africa* concludes with an interview and profile of anthropologist Richard Leakey at his Kenyan estate, where he explains his theory of sustainable conservation, the original inspiration for the show.[64]

In many ways, *Africa* offers a typical outsider's view of the continent. While the show's producers vow to avoid stereotypes by using local crews and experts to visit sensitive areas and issues, *Africa* gives every appearance of reproducing, while reworking, conventional postcolonial clichés. The show's chief protagonists are clearly first-world scientists who "discover" Africa and propel its development as a place and object of documentary inquiry. It is American and European scientists who know the continent well enough to solve its problems. And it is those scientists who are *Africa*'s real subjects, crisscrossing the land and surveilling its sites from a number of curiously lofty vantage points (including hilltops, helicopters, and even tree houses). Theirs is an authoritative (and mostly monolithic) view, compared to the sightless, silent, and mostly unreliable accounts of the local inhabitants. It is scientists alone who serve as "referees . . . bringing all sides together in matters of life and death for Africans." And it is the scientists, as represented by the show's eighteen experts (only two of whom are African) who occupy *Africa*'s most important narrative spaces—the peaceful and productive "areas of discovery" set apart, both narratively and visually, from the largely passive, violent, or exclusivist zones of African everyday life. If *Africa* has a supersubject, it is Jay Ingram, who guides us through most of the recorded locations while bridging the gap between them from a "live" home base in Kenya. It is Ingram alone who directly addresses us as viewers. And it is Ingram alone who brings us up to date on events as the sun seems to set on the story at its narrative base (the show itself was broadcast in early evening, giving Ingram's commentary all the appearance of temporal and spatial proximity). Again, it is "fly-in" experts like this who give *Africa* its intimacy, immediacy, and authority. Clearly there is a master perspective here, and it is that of outsiders.

But Africa is also represented in less predictable ways. The continent as a whole is certainly a more provisional and contested object of representation than one would expect to see in a conventional public service or domestic market documentary. Only rarely, for instance, are we presented with a fixed geographic unit whose meaning is available for straightforward documentary inquiry. Instead, Africa is repeatedly depicted as a sort of geographic mutation whose essence is elusive and perhaps nonexistent. Ingram stresses that African time is a hybrid of past and present, containing "echoes of history" while being "home to modern people as well as ancient fossils." Its space is a crisscross of rural and urban, global and local forces, with wildlife reserves, for instance, shown to be dependent on neighboring development projects "only an electric fence away" and the development efforts of sixty-eight donor nations. These juxtapositions of past and present and the proximate and the distant are underlined by rapid-fire visuals and an ever-changing world music soundtrack designed to be both "contemporary and traditional" and "generally representative" of the continent, according to the show's field producer.[65] In short, *Africa*'s occasional evolutionary and essentialist narratives are repeatedly interrupted by more complex stories of temporal and spatial flows that cross (and sometimes compromise) conventional geographic boundaries.

Further, place is also more provisional in *Africa* because it serves as a point of departure for meanings not strictly grounded in a particular territory. While the show's producers do claim to be concerned with "contemporary realities of African life," Africa the place often seems to be a trope of convenience for the Discovery network. For *@discovery.ca*, the series on which this report was aired, Africa serves as a single topic area—a sort of geographic-narrative configuration—that "encompasses the themes of the show," according to its executive producer.[66] Local scenes are superimposed on the series' rotating globe graphic. The same scenes are employed for narrative purposes throughout the show. And the same locations are made to serve as promotional vehicles for further Discovery pleasures. "What better place," asks Ingram, "to announce the birth [of the new Discovery Canada travel and culture channels] than here in one of the world's foremost travel destinations and cradles of humanity."

Finally, the pleasures of viewing a place are more ambiguous and provisional than one might expect from a conventional locally produced show. *Africa* seems to simultaneously engage our desire to know an area—our proper sense of epistophelia—and an altogether more affective and sensual set of desires. "A desire to understand [ourselves] . . . will keep bringing us back," Ingram concludes at the end of *Africa*. But this essentially pedagogical impulse is belied by the show's visual structure, the long-lingering gazes that can be read as either thoughtful reflections or exotic and even erotic attempts to capture, control, and extend our viewing of Africa and Africans. The show's field producer says *Africa* strikes an "intimate" but "confident" balance,[67] which may well appeal to both our educational and voyeuristic desires.

In all these ways, Africa is presented as an indispensable setting for a remote master narrative. This is a place to be "mined," as Ingram puts it, for facts about our past, for surprising sights and sounds, and for a range of pleasures more frequently associated with TV spectacles than conventional scientific reports. Through it all, Africa is prominent and even distinct in its way—but more as a space to be consumed by outsiders than a site to be represented for the people who live there.

Conclusion

What does this tell us, then, about global documentaries and places? To begin with, factual programs have not simply detached themselves from locations, as some cultural nationalist have forecast.[68] If anything, programmers seem to be making painstaking efforts to ground their productions in authentic ways, providing viewers with images of identifiable people, sites, and issues as part of an authentic local experience. Boundaries have not vanished and regions have not blended together on factual television, nor has documentary become a genre representing everywhere in general but nowhere in particular.

But as objects of representation, places have assumed a uniquely precarious position, certainly compared with their public service past. Consider the aggressive remodeling of places we see in documentary coproductions. Or the banal celebration (and exploitation) of places we see on the nature networks. Or the hypercommodified locations that appear in shows like *Africa*. Places survive at these sites but as means to various ends, subject to change for a variety of purposes. In the next chapter, I want to consider how this new political economy of place might affect public discussion and specifically television's tackling of issues of collective importance.

FOUR

Global Documentary
and Public Issues

Will global documentaries tackle public issues? That is, will they serve as a forum for free, equal, and more or less sensible discussions about the world? Or will they help us connect—viscerally or otherwise—with subjects beyond their own borders?

There are reasons to be both hopeful and pessimistic. For optimists, as we shall see, global documentaries might allow for investigations of collective issues—investigations that are diverse, passionate, and comprehensive, amounting to something like a "public sphere" in a digital age. For pessimists, on the other hand, global documentaries serve as a cautionary tale regarding mediated public debate: homogenizing global reports to market them in varied cultures; personalizing issues to avoid riskier public affairs topics; and often ghettoizing productions to protect channel "brands." In any of these cases, documentaries could stifle public investigations, the representation of varied points of view, and the formation of even provisional bonds among viewer-subjects in fragmented specialty markets.

Of course all of this is speculation. Arguments concerning documentary globalization tend to be short on specifics and long on theory: some informed by Habermasian models of dialogical-interpersonal communication that may not apply to mediated (particularly globally mediated) spaces,[1] and others drawing upon postmodern accounts with little to say about particular media and their contributions to public life.[2]

In this chapter I want to offer a grounded and mostly contextual analysis of documentary discussion in contemporary transnational markets. I begin with a study of constraints, including copyright laws, censorship codes, and monopoly ownership. I follow up with an examination of alternatives, including public service and independent networks that both circumvent and complement contemporary factual marketplaces. And I conclude with a look at program texts and the opportunities they hold out for public investigation on a transnational scale. My aim here is not to develop grand theories or general prescriptions. Instead I want to analyze a mix of institutional environments and program types that might (in particular circumstances) elicit some form of public response in a global documentary age.

Censorship and Global Documentary

A study of censorship is perhaps the logical place to begin such a discussion. After all, political, legal, and cultural restrictions offer the most obvious challenges to free documentary speech in a global marketplace. As documentaries cross borders, for instance, they may be subject to an increasing number of constraints in national courts and at the hands of state censors.[3] Moreover, even in a "free marketplace," documentaries may be forced to accede to the strictest community standards and prejudices of their various target markets, seeking out a lowest discursive denominator that offends, and informs, no one.[4] In all these ways, global documentaries may be subject to a sort of cumulative "public discount."

On the other hand, things may not be so simple. With regard to state and corporate censorship, one cannot easily equate the export of documentaries with a process of image filtering, especially in an era of digital processing. Digital distributors can easily re-version their products to meet the varied standards of target territories. Like many of its competitors, the Discovery network re-edits most of its programs for local sectors rather than resorting to "safe" global shows. A 1999 show on sexual arousal, for example, was made available in upright "vertical," or "talking head," versions and more explicit "horizontal," *en flagrante* (in the act) versions for different markets, and this seems to be common practice at other networks.[5] In the digital age, one-size-fits-all public affairs reports may be a thing of the past.

Satellite broadcasting may also allow distributors to negotiate, if not disregard, censorship entirely. After all, even if programmers decline to rework their programs to meet the standards of a particular market, they can sometimes sidestep those standards altogether by transmitting satellite signals that are hard to intercept by any given territory. Los Angeles–based Planet Pictures beams its productions directly into Middle East homes with the help of Middle East Television, a subsidiary of the Virginia-based Christian Broadcasting Corporation. Formal and informal gate keeping still exists in the air and on the ground, and the company operates on the assumption that "anything regarding religion, politics, sex, crime and magic" should be avoided entirely or treated carefully because of local sensibilities.[6] In a similar way, even satellite giant AOL Time Warner promised to "treat local regulations very seriously" in the wake of Chinese complaints about its CNN public affairs reports.[7] But with new delivery systems in place, documentary importers may themselves have a harder time filtering material by putting pressure on suppliers. A Discovery official says the network sees itself as responsible first and foremost to its direct to home customers. Political, cultural, and legal interference with this relationship, and various attempts on state mediation, are dealt with on a "case-by-case basis."[8]

Technically speaking, then, documentary discussions may be harder to curtail in a global age. But there are important caveats to this rule. First, it is worth remembering that technologies still work in a global cultural and regulatory environment that is often hostile to free speech without borders. We should keep in mind, for instance, that there are few actual supports, let alone guarantees, for free speech in a transnational documentary marketplace — certainly none approximating those that producers could (more or less) count on in the national public service age. True, some basic international conventions might preserve the foundations for documentary public discussion: the 1936 Geneva Convention on Propaganda, the 1952 Geneva Convention for the Right of Correction, various U.N. conventions designed to protect journalists, and perhaps most notably the 1948 Universal Declaration of Human Rights (which asserts everyone's right to receive and impart information through every medium and across every border). All of these regulations are designed to ensure, if not a transnational "public sphere," at least some minimal insurance that global citizens will be relatively well informed and not incited to kill each other.

But even in this limited sense, international regulation has had little practical effect on international communication in general and documentary programming in particular. While regional free speech provisions may occasionally override local restrictions in Europe and some other regions,[9] local laws more often than not trump international legal codes. Indeed, even in more or less liberal markets like Britain, authorities have made it clear that documentary exports are subject to the same libel, obscenity, and national security laws as their domestic counterparts. Export programs are also expected to adhere to domestic "fairness and impartiality" rules that can put a damper on unconventional documentary treatments.[10] The BBC has pledged to maintain "principles of taste and decency" and "key values of impartiality, accuracy, [and] respect for the truth" in its factual exports, thereby restricting point-of-view programming abroad much as it does at home.[11] And while some exporters may ignore domestic cultural prejudices—the Discovery sex show being a case in point—global dispensations seem to be the exception. All in all, it is probably fair to say that global productions enjoy few of the supports and many of the restrictions of their domestic counterparts. In this respect, global documentaries have been deprived of a safe public sphere.

In other ways, documentary censorship is not just possible but probable in a global age. For a start, documentaries may be filtered at the inception stage by subjects and sources who, like their producer counterparts, find them to be riskier forums than domestic programs. Scientists around the world, for instance, may be more reluctant to speak out on controversial issues such as animal testing because of their fear of transnational protests.[12] At the same time, producers and distributors may be wary of tackling controversial issues because of pressure from powerful interested parties. Multinational drug and biotech companies, for instance, have reportedly managed to curb documentary investigations of the genetically modified food industry.[13] Government authorities also have sought to influence documentary debates, as in a 2002 White House "information" conference when international current affairs reporting was deemed to be "fraught with risks and possibilities" in the wake of the September 11 attacks.[14]

Of course, pressure tactics and stonewalling are nothing new for documentary filmmakers. But in a transnational market, they may be easier to target and more worth targeting, and globalization perhaps makes them more vulnerable than ever. In all these ways, globalization seems to have made the consequences of public discourse incalculable for producers, subjects, and regulators alike. Documentary investigation is simply riskier than ever for all parties. For these reasons, "ethical risk assessments"—of the sort proposed by some critics in domestic markets[15]—may be simply impractical at the global level. As one producer notes, participants are less likely to speak out in global documentaries "because they don't know where the words are going."[16]

All in all then, public discussion is only relatively possible in a global documentary age. To be sure, many productions have managed to circumvent censors and morph themselves into ever-changing free-market products that elude conventional regulatory controls. But mobile and mutable as they may be, documentaries continue to face a number of borders and barriers that seem to be globally endemic and that often shape the projects at inception. "These are the best and worst of times for documentary," says independent producer Philip Hampson. "There have never been so many ways to make a difference, and never so many practical difficulties doing that."[17]

Concentration and Global Documentary

And what about corporate censorship in a global marketplace? That is, will documentary play host to a range of ideas even if dominated by an ever-smaller group of corporate players? Again there are reasons to be both hopeful and optimistic. The risk of corporate constraint, and thus uniformity, is certainly real insofar as the documentary industry has been taken over by a small group of producers and distributors, each with at least the potential of putting its stamp on outgoing product. In France, for instance, the top thirty-six producers now account for more than 50 percent of the country's output, capping a trend toward documentary centralization in the past decade. The industry is even more concentrated in the United Kingdom, with the top 12 production companies controlling more than 80 percent of market earnings, and the top fifty earning 90 percent of independent commissions, by one estimate.[18] The situation is somewhat different in Canada, where independent producers are numerous, dispersed, and often insignificant as market players (global or otherwise).[19] But in most countries, viable producers are becoming fewer in number, with possible repercussions for public discourse.

Domestic consolidation may be exacerbated by global monopolization and new types of capital flows. Documentary buyers—particularly big global satellite channels—sometimes drive small producers out of business by demanding domestic and international rights to programs that are an important source of income for their makers. Discovery, for instance, typically demands full global and domestic rights in exchange for 50 percent funding at the production stage,[20] which makes growth hard to sustain for many of its independent suppliers. Consolidation may be further reinforced by deregulatory policies, as liberalized investment rules allow for global takeovers such as that of TVNZ's Natural History Unit by Rupert Murdoch's News Corporation. With many signatories to the General Agreement on Trade in Services (GATS) waiving their long-standing restrictions on cultural imports and investment, the emergence of international production monopolies is a real possibility in the near future.[21]

Consolidation is also taking place at the distribution level, and again, this seems to be exacerbated by global monopoly practices. Independent distributor Jane Balfour Productions, for instance, was long a haven for social issue documentaries but went bankrupt in 2000 partly because of competition from the new distribution arms of the larger global channels.[22] In many respects, the marketing and making of documentaries is no longer a small player's game.

Finally, consolidation is reinforced by vertical integration, much as it has been by concentration at all levels of production. Integration can involve the consolidation of diverse operations, as has been the case with Discovery's new distribution efforts. Or it may involve buyouts of documentary channels themselves by outside players like cable distributors or larger cultural conglomerates, such as the purchase of major shares of A&E and the History Channel by Disney Corporation and General Electric, respectively, in the late 1990s.[23] Arguably, this trend more than any other makes documentary diversity hard to sustain in a global marketplace. It is because of integration pressures that cable companies around the world are working to acquire factual television channels and give them preferential treatment on their own services. It is also because of these pressures that broadcasters are seeking to own documentary programs and thus benefit from global syndication instead of simply licensing them in pursuit of domestic advertising revenues.

All in all, these trends make the whole idea of dynamic independent production problematic. The takeover of documentary projects by distributors and programmers has become a fact of life in many markets. One recent example is the 2000 acquisition of one of Canada's main independent producers, Great North Communications, by one of its largest film and television distributors, Alliance-Atlantis, and the subsequent launch of the Independent Film and Documentary Channel, a co-venture of the latter with the BBC, News Corporation, and National Geographic. Another is the 2000 takeover of the United Kingdom's largest independent producer, Menton Barraclough Clarey, by one of that country's largest distributors. Trade magazine writer Mary Ellen Armstrong has noted that "nichecasters" and networks around the world are purchasing production companies and "corralling talent in a way that would do Hollywood proud."[24] Canadian specialty channel executive Bill Roberts says this may result in smaller channels being "marginalized as communication conglomerates [begin to] own content."[25] TCI's recent threat to remove The Learning Channel from its U.S. cable packages in the wake of an unsuccessful takeover bid highlights the dangers of integrated factual distribution of this sort. It also suggests that documentary offerings may be fewer and more familiar in years to come.[26]

A narrowing of documentary range is also apparent in integrated production systems. The tendency for programs to be produced by programmers as part of a single corporate package is becoming more evident in a number of markets. In the public service sector, the BBC's closing of its Independent Commissioning Group and its establishment of output guarantees for its own production department are perhaps a sign of things to come. In the private sector, channels like Canal Plus that used to purchase independent productions have shifted toward in-house series programming to take advantage of economies of scale.[27] In both sectors, global competition seems to be resulting in "Fordist" modes of retrenchment.

Independents will probably survive in these conditions, but they may be more vulnerable. To be sure, larger programmers claim the industry cannot survive without content from outside the corporate core. Indeed, the world's largest documentary producer, DNI, claims it will remain a showcase for independent work, leaving over 90 percent of its schedule open to outside, unaffiliated bids.[28] But in many sectors of the industry, the trend toward corporate control and only marginal independent input is clear, with few obstacles in its way.

And what about government regulations that might force the industry to open its doors to marginalized perspectives? The indications as yet are that ownership and content policies will do little to stem the monopoly tide. Indeed, many domestic regulations facilitate, if not actively encourage, monopoly production practices. Canadian independent production policies, for instance, allow networks and nichecasters to soak up government-sponsored "diversity" funds. Broadcasters thus use affiliated companies to access their quota of 33 percent of the Canadian Television Fund while controlling, through their commissions from independents, fully 87 percent of that fund.[29] Publicly subsidized documentaries are thus overwhelmingly dominated by big players. At the same time, regulations designed to encourage diverse documentary perspectives often exacerbate corporate consolidation by favoring larger broadcaster-connected firms that are able to invest a substantial amount of their own capital in productions and that have received a prime-time scheduling commitment from domestic or international broadcasters.[30] Government policies have had a similar effect in Australia, where the Film Finance

Corporation favors more experienced applicants with industry ties.[31] One observer has actually likened funding agencies like these to "banks" that look favorably on investment projects, especially those with international partners.[32]

With policy supports like these, today's documentary industry has increasingly taken the form of a Hollywood studio system, with large and often vertically integrated production houses affiliating themselves with established network conglomerates and a small number of producers still in business but mostly dependent on these players.[33] This hardly constitutes a free marketplace of documentary ideas.

Finally, there seems to be less and less competition among producers left standing in this sort of marketplace. Recent co-ventures between the world's largest documentary players certainly suggest a trend toward monopolistic collaboration over competitive diversity. A 1998 deal between the BBC and Discovery, for instance, provides for more than US$665 million worth of coproduction and cross-promotions around the world, and while the BBC's stated desire to "dominate factual viewing in every corner of the globe" appears to have been wishful thinking—the global documentary market has hardly been locked up by either partner—a recent investigation by the European Community does suggest the venture could withdraw a good deal of source material by effectively tying up image archives around the world.[34] Not only is the documentary industry concentrated, then—it seems to be dominated by a small number of powerful players who may, for one reason or another, offer similar images of the world in documentary form.

Copyright and Global Documentary

But perhaps the most serious threat to documentary diversity involves not corporate or political censorship per se, but seemingly innocuous laws concerning the ownership of images. On the one hand, factual source material seems more available

than ever. New data systems such as the Image Bank promise eventual desktop access to complete footage archives.[35] Online stores such as the Documentary News Net offer more than
10,000 documentaries and 3 million titles in conjunction with
Amazon.com, while catalogues like the International Documentary Source Book list more than 14,000 programs and films
in seventy-nine topic areas.[36] While these facilities are now
only available in Europe, North America, and parts of Asia,
they may become ubiquitous as even "marginal" collections
like Russia's Krasnagorsk archives undergo digitalization. The
world's images are hardly instantly or evenly accessible, but
they do seem to be more accessible than ever in today's digital
market.

But again, the technical possibilities of "free flow" may
clash with the political and economic realities of the global
marketplace. Indeed in many ways, restrictions on the circulation of images have tended to increase in the wake of
digital globalization. Rights for global digital footage can be
enormously expensive compared with rights for national analog footage. British Pathe charges about US$100 a second for
global rights compared with about US$15 for local service.[37]
Moreover, as footage goes global, more and more claimants
demand a stake in ownership of its various parts, including
music, pictures, and even recognizable locations. Even the Empire State Building now collects license fees from documentary
producers, and in these circumstances fewer and fewer of the
world's objects and ideas may be available for a free documentary airing.

Rights are not only more expensive but more complicated
in a global digital market, and this may further hinder the
movement of material across borders. Parties must now negotiate revenues and fees for new territories, new media, and
new viewer groups—one example being the "trapped audience" rights sector that governs programs in airport lounges
and the like. At the same time, image ownership itself is increasingly unclear. In the United States, even material in the

public domain seems to be vulnerable in the wake of a recent U.S. Superior Court decision granting some of the rights to the federally owned Kennedy assassination footage to its original owners. As for privately owned stock, less than 10 percent of archive houses give producers an accurate idea of the rights attached to a particular clip, according to one recent estimate.[38] Facing risks like these, producers must hire agents to gain clearance, or simply avoid unknown footage altogether. More than ever, the world's sights, sounds, and concepts seem to be tied up in intellectual property disputes.

The situation is exacerbated by a variety of monopoly tactics and bureaucratic maneuvers in the state and corporate sectors. Some institutions steal documentary material, laying claim to all sorts of stray footage, particularly from third world areas, no matter what the actual source.[39] Others hoard documentary images; DNI, for instance, reserves archive material for its own producers, and powerful sources like the Beatles buy up all known footage of themselves for exclusive, licensed use.[40] Even speaking subjects can be monopolized, with more superchannels concluding exclusive deals with sources and the National Geographic channel "sign[ing] up as many scientists as possible" for its special reports.[41] Still other documentary producers and regulators destroy footage: the former Taliban government of Afghanistan nearly eliminated the country's film and television archives,[42] while less infamously, archive houses around the world discard material not of interest to affluent clients to save on costs of digital transfer.[43] In these cases, global technologies have led to the wholesale withdrawal of images and ideas from documentary circulation. In the face of rising costs, increasing paperwork, and a shrinking public archive, more producers may rely on less documentary material, with the result that one sees "the same kind of stuff turn up on cable stations over and over again."[44]

A number of legal quirks may restrict the movement of documentary images, with similarly devastating results. Existing copyright regimes hardly facilitate a free flow of programming across borders, if only because U.S. copyright laws are notoriously out of sync with those of the rest of the world (the United States did not sign on to international agreements in this area until 1955, much later than most countries).[45] Europe is making belated efforts to make its copyright laws regionally coherent based on the fairly restrictive (rights holder-friendly) rules prevailing in France and Germany, but before the deals are done, the transfer of documentary footage within and between regions will be complex and costly. At the moment, North American producers can claim "fair use" of footage at home but not in Europe, where more restrictive rules prevail, while in the United Kingdom, producers can claim rights for "educational use" not available in other parts of the world.[46] Not surprisingly, a recent factual television study concludes that conflicting copyright rules are a "disincentive for the export of domestic programs."[47]

It is mostly for these reasons that the world's ideas and images are less "public" than ever. To be sure, efforts are being made to change this situation in a global documentary age. The U.K.-based company Survivor Films, for instance, helps filmmakers, nongovernmental organizations (NGOs), and third world communities "who never get access to [environmental] footage just because they can't afford it."[48] Similarly, the U.K.-based company World Images works on behalf of clients including Greenpeace and the Red Cross that are "taking a hard look at world issues."[49] Meanwhile, the U.S.-based International Wildlife Film Festival operates a Robin Hood Fund that gives revenues and even footage from "blue-chip" nature shows to NGOs and filmmakers in third world countries. But more often than not, global images are effectively managed by corporate and state interests for whom free flow is an afterthought. Now more than ever, documentary is controlled and commodified at source, making it a precarious public domain in principle.

Public Programming and Global Documentary

But what about documentary in practice, and specifically the programs we see on television or in cinemas? That is, if documentary production is subject to new constraints, what impact has this had on documentary texts? This is a complex question, as the connection between corporate control and content is not as straightforward as one might think. Consider monopolized image markets, for instance, where producers make the best of a bad situation by drawing upon older archive material in surprising new ways. Or, better still, imagine filmmakers avoiding the stock market entirely in favor of footage they record themselves for altogether new sorts of productions. Indeed, one could easily argue that copyright and consolidation problems will spark a renaissance in new documentaries, or at least "recombinant" filmmaking.[50] In these cases, we cannot simply concur with predictions that "the same kind of stuff [will] turn up on cable stations over and over again."[51] This view fails to account for the resourcefulness of documentary producers in ever-changing circumstances. It fails to account, that is, for documentary producers as agents.

That said, the verdict on market documentaries and their public potential has been largely negative, at least among academic observers. Dominated by a few transnational, profit-driven players, factual television in general and documentary television in particular is often assumed to be homogeneous, personalized, and sensationalistic. In this section, I want to consider these arguments in more detail to determine what can be said about documentary's public potential beyond market analysis per se.

The arguments concerning the sameness of global programs should be considered first, as they seem to follow logically from what we know about factual monopolies. In simple categorical terms, topic diversity is easy to assess—one can simply look at the number of programs at major festivals that fit into self-defined types. By this measure, documentary production actually seems to be quite diverse. Program range at the commercial MIP, for instance, is surprisingly wide and eclectic, at least if one accepts the program categories used by the industry itself (see chapter 2). Recent market reports indicate not just a broad mix of productions but fluid fashion trends such that no single program type dominates the industry over time. It is also worth noting that in some markets the steady demand for nature shows and docusoaps seems to have abated in favor of arts, culture, history, and current affairs programming—genres traditionally associated with public affairs television.[52] According to a recent study, this sort of fare now accounts for 60 percent of the hours and 65 percent of the budgets of global documentary today.[53]

In terms of straight subject matter, then, documentaries seem to be varied and at least conceivably "public." But stylistic diversity is harder to measure, and here there seems to be a good deal of cause for concern. Canadian studies indicate a drop-off in stand-alone feature productions, where eclectic point-of-view styles would seem to be most likely.[54] Meanwhile, European critics warn somewhat more amorphously of a decline in documentary "creativity" in favor of cautious, "corporate" factual formulas.[55]

Though these claims are hard to assess, the assertion that a concentrated industry yields only corporatized "McDocs"—bland, uniform, risk-free products that please and inform no one—can be questioned on political-economic grounds alone. In fact, far from seeking only conservative and monolithic programming, most firms develop what from their point of view is a rationally eclectic lineup where "alternative" productions may loom large. Time Warner's HBO channel, for instance, supports "edge" products—programs whose revenue depends on their precise demographic appeal and the willingness of viewers to pay for them "because that's what they really want."[56] Discovery similarly accepts "specialized" documentaries with crossover potential while funding "social component" programs, particularly concerning the environment, that can be leveraged into other sectors.[57] Other buyers find that edge productions create spin-off opportunities in ancillary markets, which have become an increasing source of revenue for rights holders around the world.[58]

While much of this material is edited for broadcast, many independent producers say their work is shown with less interference on superchannels than on the smaller counterparts. A filmmaker at the environmentally based Asterisk Productions of Victoria, British Columbia, says her work has been shown on Discovery "largely intact."[59] In short, at least a limited range of diversity may be possible in the global market, given the multiple circuits of communication in which its products—even its monopoly products—now circulate. Decision makers at most superchannels apparently believe their companies can make more money from a diverse documentary portfolio than from a standardized global repertoire.

If anything, a sameness of documentary styles—insofar as it exists—may result from competition rather than monopolies. The voracious demand for nichecaster programs, for instance, results in lower license fees, particularly in peripheral markets such as Latin America. While programmers bought more documentaries than ever in 2000, investments in the genre actually declined by about one-third partly because of economies of scale and technological gains, but mostly because of lower broadcaster payments and faster production turnarounds.[60] Declining revenues in turn make it necessary for "product" to be turned out at an unprecedented rate, which may discourage any sort of experimentation or critical self-reflection on the part of producers. In today's "free" market, many documentary makers admit they must "decide what a story is going to be ahead of time, write it, get the experts and add the pictures because it's easier to shoot that way."[61] This is an oftcited problem in documentary production today, but it hardly results from censorship or consolidation per se.

The situation may be exacerbated by other free-market forces such as the hypercompetitive branding efforts of specialty buyers. In an effort to distinguish themselves from their peers, many services seek to confine and contain their products within commercially convenient categories—within a more or less fixed "slot." Even officials at Vision TV, reputedly one of Canada's more daring and diverse specialty channels, insist that programs conform to its religious-humanist "hatch, match, and dispatch" mandate. In short, a good degree of uniformity is evident in today's documentary industry, but it can be attributed to more or less open markets as well as monopoly "distortions."

We should be wary, then, of corporate standardization forecasts just as we should of apocalyptic claims concerning corporate dumbing down and "copping out." For Dovey, documentary markets give rise to the docusoap, which is essentially "inert as a public service form."[62] For Zimmermann, global market schedules are dominated by "celebrity profiles . . . and wild animal programs," and serious public affairs investigation is not welcome.[63] For Robins, market documentaries offer a sort of privatized postmodern spectacle—"sensation without responsibility"—consisting of controlled shocks that can be mastered and screened out by image consumers.[64] In all of these scenarios, the public service effort to inform and empower viewers has been effectively undermined by crass commercial antics and deeper structural forces.

But there are reasons to question all of these critiques. First of all, the idea that personalized documentaries are inherently "unpublic" is somewhat problematic, at least as a general model of factual programming. It is worth remembering that many "subjective" documentaries are a well-established tradition in public discourse, held in high regard at the height of the national public service age. For the 1948 World Union of Documentary, documentaries would ideally "appeal to reason and emotion" with the help of such tactics as "sincere and justifiable reconstruction."[65] For Marshall McLuhan and Quentin Fiore, writing in the 1960s, factual programming should "pour upon us instantly and continuously the concerns of other men [*sic*]"—largely through "acoustic" and affective styles that eschew more sober modes of public address.[66] Assertions that programs like these preclude either information or empathy are thus questionable if one takes past public service perspectives into account.

Contemporary developments further call into question the above-mentioned critiques. "Screening" critiques are perhaps most persuasive with regard to global texts, as it may indeed be the case that highly packaged images of distant events allow for an "intoxication of the senses" at one remove, as Robins and others imply. Bauman's recent assertion that global travel and public affairs shows allow "tele-tourists" to both consume and contain threatening images of third and fourth world inhabitants makes intuitive sense.[67] Indeed, transnational reports sometimes seem designed for "tuned-out" viewing in which the world is simultaneously engaged and ignored in a very unpublic sort of way. Personalized documentaries in particular seem to offer "closed worlds" and "stock characters" with which we could never have a real sense of connection. Or they may provide us with narcotic "fields of play" that indulge our most infantile and antisocial fantasies. But such theories certainly need backing up.

In the meantime, there are several problems with these views as they stand. Empirically, the evidence that documentary has become a first-person genre is somewhat mixed. Studies in the United Kingdom do suggest that "international documentary" reports give short shrift to the world's social problems, focusing instead on British celebrities and contestants in exotic locales. A recent U.K. study finds that "harder issue-focused programmes have been reduced to unprecedented low levels," while "softer, more accessible and entertainment-led formats now dominate."[68] But against these findings, some international reports suggest an upturn in science, arts, and educational programs at the expense of "sensationalistic" reality and travel shows (though information and entertainment may converge in both of the latter categories, of course). Certainly the idea that documentaries simply bypass public issues is empirically disputable if we take a range of program markets into account.[69]

Second, the strategic and conceptual underpinnings of market critiques are questionable. Some "spectacle" critiques can be read as nostalgic endorsements of sober public service programming that may not have been very public in the first place. By some accounts, Griersonian documentaries rarely let subjects speak and rarely motivated them as actors in the world at large. It is perhaps no surprise, then, that contemporary documentaries that take a similarly "distant and difficult" approach to world issues fail to inspire viewers who do not "get" or do not want to "get" their message.[70] The challenge for contemporary documentary would seem to be to connect two worlds—the abstract "global" and the proximate, everyday "local"[71]—and this is a problem about which conventional public service documentaries, and the critiques inspired by them, have little to say.

Finally, as we noted above, many image market critiques are largely speculative and devoid of ethnographic support. It is at least conceivable, for instance, that documentary spectacles, particularly violent spectacles, provoke something more than smug European feelings of mastery and control among viewers in documentary's peripheral markets. As much as "screening" responses are eagerly anticipated (usually by disapproving European experts), viewers may well respond to global documentaries in less predictable ways on the ground. At the very least, first world critics would be well advised to differentiate between those global viewers whose "experience of violence is mediated and those living within the orbit of the constant threat of its eruption," as Nick Stevenson has put it in another context.[72] In short, criticisms of documentary sensationalism are often more presumptive than ethnographic and only superficially grounded in the actual life worlds of documentary viewers today.[73]

So if the evidence concerning markets, texts, and viewers is ambivalent, what are the chances for public discourse in a global documentary age? Probably irredeemably mixed. Taking institutional and ethnographic evidence into account, documentary public discussion is perhaps best seen as conceivable but conditional in today's marketplace. Neither market critics nor market advocates help us weigh the possibilities in this regard, offering in their more optimistic and apocalyptic versions all-or-nothing scenarios in which public spheres either disappear or survive intact in new institutional environments. In actual fact, it seems fair to say that the new political economies of factual television are neither inherently hostile nor naturally conducive to free expression in the documentary genre. Instead they seem to create fleeting public spaces that deserve careful scrutiny and conditional support.

Public Service Broadcasting and Global Documentary

Where else might we look for a documentary public sphere beyond the market per se? We might start with the national public service channels that despite a decline in funds and viewership still remain a significant source and destination for documentaries around the world. To be sure, there are signs that the public service commitment to "serious" documentaries is waning. The Australian Broadcasting Corporation has made deep cuts to current affairs and documentary programming since 2000,[74] while the Brazilian public broadcaster TV Cultura reduced its own domestic documentaries to 100 hours a year, compared with 270 hours of foreign programs in 2001.[75] Even in Europe, the heartland of the public service documentary tradition, broadcasters like ARD and ZDF in Germany have been criticized for shortchanging the genre in favor of more lucrative sports events.[76] In the United Kingdom, the BBC has taken itself to task for its preoccupation with "lighter" factual material at the same time that the private networks have been widely criticized on similar grounds.[77] Meanwhile, budget cuts have forced public broadcasters like Ireland's RTE to contract out most of their productions and reduce their schedules to just a few shows a week.[78] In many respects, the public service commitment to documentary seems to be faltering.

But if there are cracks in the edifice, we should remember that public broadcasters have been uniquely supportive of documentary programming over the years and, in key areas, continue to be so today. Public service broadcasters still account for much of the value and the volume of documentary production (though exactly how much remains unclear). One study suggests that generalist channels account for 41 percent of market value and 70 percent of market volume worldwide (though how many of these are public service programs per se is not specified).[79] Moreover, archive holdings alone guarantee public institutions a prominent place in the documentary industry for years to come, with public service libraries remaining the largest in the world. Further, as exhibitors, public service channels offer one of the last prime-time venues for long-form documentaries around the world in countries as far apart as India and Canada.[80] And as transnational investors and distributors, public service channels continue to play an important role in the global marketplace. The European Broadcasting Union's funding of international co-productions—on the grounds that "only the BBC and the German and French broadcasters can survive doing big budget documentaries by themselves"[81]—shows the determination of public service organizations to compete in an international marketplace.[82] Bilateral and multilateral arrangements have also opened up new markets, with recent co-ventures between PBS, the BBC, and various market players, making public service programs perhaps more commercially viable than ever.[83] Finally, new global distribution projects may ensure a lasting digital presence, with ZDF launching ZDF.doku and the BBC planning a number of factual satellite channels of its own.[84] All in all, public service documentaries may be more visible than ever on global television, albeit in a more competitive environment.

Recent initiatives by the Canadian Broadcasting Corporation illustrate this variegated approach and its potential and pitfalls. Domestically the CBC has tried to raise its profile by diversifying output and establishing prime-time slots for independent long-form documentaries. The *Rough Cuts* series, for instance, promises to open up the airwaves to "creative new perspectives not always available in television journalism." At the same time, the CBC has bankrolled national megaprojects like the 2001 *Canada: A People's History*, the "largest [and most expensive] photographic survey of Canada," according to its producers.[85] Transnationally the CBC has attempted to boost exports and "fight for documentaries in this most Darwinian of [international] broadcast markets."[86] The CBC has coproduced (with Channel 4) globally themed shows such as the 1996 *Dawn of the Eye* concerning news and current affairs reporting around the world. The CBC also has arranged for worldwide distribution of its regular shows, securing a slot on the U.S.-based DirecTV satellite service, through which public affairs programs like *the fifth estate* can be seen by more than 2.5 million American and international viewers.[87]

But along the way, CBC documentaries have encountered a number of commercial and cultural glitches. Domestically the CBC is a much-diminished cultural institution, exerting less influence than ever on Canadian productions and styles. Part of the problem is its dwindling resources. "A decade ago, CBC News had 10 documentary teams geared to the national news agenda," notes a documentary executive producer. "Now there are none."[88] And while the CBC plans to set up a new permanent documentary unit in the wake of its ratings success with *Canada: A People's History*, early dreams of a publicly subsidized, coast-to-coast documentation project—dreams on which public service programming was founded in Canada— seem more distant than ever. Instead, the CBC has yielded much of its domestic market share to the specialty channels; it accounted for just 22 percent of documentary investment in Canada in 1998–1999, compared with 60 percent just seven years earlier.[89] This is a more dramatic reversal of fortune than that suffered by its European counterparts, but it is still indicative of a gradual worldwide trend toward independent production and nichecasting in the documentary business.

In purely cultural terms, the CBC has found its job harder to do as well, at least in a traditional sense. The CBC's adherence to a general public service model of factual broadcasting—and its insistence that local productions adhere to conventional journalistic notions of free ("fair and balanced") expression and "general" interest and appeal—has proved increasingly unsatisfactory for a number of viewers and producers. And while the CBC has promised to change with the times—opening its doors to local producers and taking "risks with newcomers" in the age of the specialty channel—it still insists that all programs "explore themes crucial to all Canadians" while adhering to "traditional CBC editorial [standards of] journalistic excellence,"[90] an approach that has led to "excessive caution and buck passing" at the commissioning stage, according to some critics.[91]

Advocates argue that the CBC is more relevant than ever as a forum for marginalized cultures in ratings-driven markets. To be sure, the CBC probably addresses cultural difference more effectively than it did in the public service Golden Age, when minority communities were either dismissed or rendered invisible as generically "modern" subjects. But the CBC still seems a bit skittish and even dated in its multicultural endeavors.

Most important, minorities tend to be ghettoized as "special interest" categories, a pattern all too common on public service television.[92] The BBC, for instance, often marginalizes minority points of view by requiring balance when "issues involved are highly controversial and a defining or decisive cultural moment is imminent."[93] The Independent Television Commission (ITC), for its part, enforces restrictive notions of public service balance in British broadcasting (at least "if it is not likely that the licensee will soon return to the subject").[94] Similarly, the Australian Broadcasting Corporation calls for the presentation of "principal relevant viewpoints on matters of importance," either within a single program or within a "reasonable period."[95] These requirements impose an onerous burden of representation on minorities by forcing them to remove "marginal" perspectives in favor of "principal viewpoints." In even worse-case scenarios, minority perspectives may fall outside the balance scale altogether as broadcasters like India's

Doordarshan service air only those "regional" documentaries found to be in the "national interest."[96] In short, public service programming may have suffered not just because of dwindling resources but because of entrenched and questionable representation practices.

There are, of course, alternatives to public broadcasting as we have defined it, and they may hold out hope for documentary discussion in a novel form. Certainly, a number of local and transnational projects allow for less monolithic sorts of public discourse than those mentioned above. PBS' Independent Television Service (ITVS) supports "creative risks and . . . underserved populations" in documentary programming,[97] though recent attacks by conservative groups suggest that free speech is far from secure in these officially sanctioned public spaces.[98] Britain's Channel 4 similarly eschews a general-interest audience strategy and includes a number of local point-of-view programs in its lineup,[99] though its proprietary stance toward rights and license fees calls its own commitment to diverse independent production into question. Some producers also have noted a growing hostility to "special interest" documentaries at many of these channels, particularly concerning environmental topics.[100]

Another documentary alternative is the independent service sector producing and distributing public stories across borders. The Television Trust for the Environment, for instance, describes itself as an "independent broker" between NGOs and established broadcasters, circumventing some of the more restrictive forms of mediation in documentary distribution sectors. At the same time, the trust acknowledges its limitations in this respect, noting that many local environmental programs "don't travel well," while larger issues like global warming are "regarded warily" by ratings-conscious broadcasters.[101] And while the trust sees its audience to be "truly worldwide," it concedes that, so far, audiences have responded more readily to proximate and personal programs than to "serious global investigations."[102] In short, independent services seem to acknowledge the limitations of their own project and the difficulties of fostering "global solidarity and mutual concern" through documentary programming[103] (an issue I will address in chapter 5).

Other notable "alternative" approaches include Australia's Special Broadcasting Service, which appeals to grounded but dispersed diasporic communities within and beyond Australia's borders. SBS offers postnational "snapshots" of the nation, "creatively communicating the values, the voices, and the visions of multicultural Australia and the contemporary world."[104] The service is perhaps best seen as a common carrier with some editorial functions, allowing emerging social formations rather than fixed special interests the opportunity to come together and express a changing cultural identity over time. Here documentation is conceived as a process rather than a product. That is, SBS' programs are designed as "encounters" rather than finished documents, portraits of community interaction that often call the identities of all participants into question.[105]

Less predictable types of free speech are also evident at Canada's Vision TV, a specialty channel described as the "only multi-faith religious broadcaster" in the world,[106] actively encouraging dialogues between religious groups in lieu of a more segregated special-interest approach. At the same time, Vision's programs are deliberately self-reflexive rather than merely expressive of a set point of view. Like SBS, Vision creates spaces for "identity formation." "Our programs explore changing faith and ways of living through dialogue," explains a channel spokesman.[107]

Finally, worth considering are the myriad film and video documentary projects intended to define collective issues in new ways. Take, for example, the avowedly anti-globalization video cooperatives working under the umbrella of the Indymedia Documentation Project, put together to document (and mobilize) viewers against globalization with the help of North American media collectives like Whispered Media, Deep Dish TV, and Paper Tiger TV and a number of native rights documentary groups. All of these organizations take a determinedly critical stance toward the global economy, but most deal with commercial cable and satellite carriers to make sure their productions reach a worldwide audience. As such, Indymedia offers a challenge to "mainstream" documentary markets, but it hardly constitutes a full-fledged alternative to the global documentary industry.

The same can be said of independent filmmakers who have managed to find a new audience for social justice documentaries around the world. The recent box-office success of films like *Fahrenheit 911* and *Control Room* has led many observers to foretell a new type of alternative documentary cinema, opposed to mainstream themes and commercial marketing strategies. But we should be cautious here. Many of these films have been aggressively promoted by some of the world's largest film distributors such as Miramax while also helping give rise to a new type of auteur-star system in the documentary industry. Marketing trends like these both enable and constrain independent filmmakers like Michael Moore or Jehane Noujaim. That is, global markets allow them to reach larger audiences than ever while at the same time exposing them to commercial pressures reminiscent of the television ratings system. As one distributor put it, if critical filmmakers "don't perform by a second screening Sunday they're off the screen."[108] In other words, the fate of independent documentary continues to depend in large part on the vagaries of global capital cycles, and a growing number of filmmakers struggle to reach audiences under these conditions.

None of these documentary strategies offers a single, irreproachable model for public discourse. Indeed the very concept of alternative documentary, somehow outside or above the global marketplace, is increasingly problematic in the hypercommodified world of factual programming. But together, broadcasters, narrowcasters, distributors, and producers have developed innovative ways of representing the world, calling into question categorical public service and market models. These new types remind us that free speech in a global age is possible but only provisionally "guaranteed" by any one institutional arrangement. In this respect, documentarists do indeed face the best and worst of times, calling for critical and contextual investigation rather than grand (and often banal) theory building.

An Example: *Haunted Land*

If the shape of public infrastructure is uncertain, what might public programs look like in a global age? That is, how might new forms of transnational broadcasting translate into new types of public texts? In this section, I want to examine in detail one case, which, while hardly covering all the formal options, does suggest some ways public affairs discourse might be reformulated in a postnational era.

Haunted Land is an instructive case. Produced in Canada and designed for distribution on international film and television markets, this one-hour piece examines human rights abuses in Guatemala and international efforts to redress them. *Haunted Land* begins with an image of a village obscured by mountain mist, which serves as the visual motif of right-wing genocide in Central America. Mateo Pablo, the film's narrator and a former inhabitant, explains that he was forced to flee in 1982 because of army atrocities supported at least indirectly by the U.S. government. The film follows him on his first trip back to the village, accompanied by Daniel Hernandez-Salazar, a Guatemalan photographer and archivist, and Sarah Baillargeon, an international refugee activist representing Quebec-based Projet Accompagnement.

As *Haunted Land* unfolds, Hernandez-Salazar's and Baillargeon's roles in the film become clearer. For the former, Mateo's return is an "exercise in memory"—in short supply in Guatemala and around the world, where accounts of the thirty-six-year civil war are generally met with repression or indifference. Baillargeon, for her part, wants to help Mateo in "an emotional process" and, of course, prevent him from being killed. The challenge for both activists, and the film crew, will be to "share this experience with others," which Hernandez-Salazar explains is "never easy." A previous observer, Guatemalan bishop Juan Gerardi, was murdered just two days after releasing a human rights report on the massacres in 1998. The photographer's own pictures have been repeatedly censored by local militias. Meanwhile, support work going on in refugee centers in Quebec and in various visual archive centers suffers from lack of funds and government support. Mateo's own journey to his village is torturous, and the testimonials from its remaining inhabitants are muted and cautious. The film concludes with scenes of site excavations and skull counts as Hernandez-Salazar tries to put the event in some sort of traumatized visual perspective.

Ultimately, *Haunted Land* can be seen as a film about witnessing. Repeatedly our attention is drawn to the difficulty of recording and remembering events—particularly those removed from most viewers in space and time. For Mateo the "past is obscured by clouds" as he "reencounters" his native land in a perilous whirlwind tour. For Hernandez-Salazar the past is an "open wound" that must be handled with care. And for Baillargeon it is the "property of others" that can be comprehended but only in the "fleeting moments" of its traces. Indeed, the monumental events being recorded—the murder of more than 200,000 Guatemalans from 1954 to 1990—seem to defy comprehension, a fact underlined by the film's restless montage of foreign and domestic settings and historical and contemporary imagery.

But this is not just a film about epistemology and its limits. *Haunted Land* can also be read as a cautionary tale concerning global image markets and the constraints they place on public witnessing. In fact, the film was never accepted for broadcast, never even picked up by an international distributor. *Haunted Land* was screened at a number of third world and native film festivals in 2001, after which it disappeared from the global marketplace without a trace.

The reasons for this may have had much to do with the nature of documentary globalization itself. According to the film's producer, Mary Ellen Davis, what broadcasters inside and outside Canada found hard to accept was not so much the subject matter of the film but the "intimacy" of its approach—particularly its insistence on letting "foreign" subjects speak at length, and in personal terms, about their own lives and circumstances. Commissioners who found the topic interesting believed "professionals" could tackle it more "objectively." The French-language public service television network, Societe Radio-Canada, sent its own team to cover the Gerardi murder just two days after receiving the *Haunted Land* pitch.[109] In other words, broadcasters could only accommodate "foreign" stories told by domestic reporters in properly distant (either "authoritative" or "sensationalistic") terms. It was by these means—and these means alone—that the market could make the "global" local.

So what does this tell us about public discourse in a global documentary age? In this instance, it was precisely the effort to make distant people and abstract events "familiar" and "human"—precisely the approach endorsed by many contemporary film global media theorists—that made *Haunted Land* unacceptable for global programmers, even those ostensibly committed to an internationalist agenda. For global broadcasters, there is "nothing intimate about foreign stories," according to Davis.[110] For most, the world outside their own markets remains a distant and inaccessible place.

Conclusion

Such cautionary tales remind us that documentary free speech is hardly absolute in a global age. Industry consolidation is rampant, copyright restrictions endemic, and buying practices insular and chauvinistic, reducing the depth and range of documentary images by most measures and for most viewers around the world. Global documentaries remain subject to many of the restrictions and few of the supports of the national public service era. At the same time, new spaces for producing and viewing these programs—spaces peculiar to the new political economy of television and film—promise new types of collective discourse that may be fleeting and unfamiliar but worthy of critical support nonetheless. In the next chapter I want to examine these spheres of practice more closely and consider how, within them, documentaries might continue to "mean" something in a global age.

FIVE

Global Documentary
and Meaning

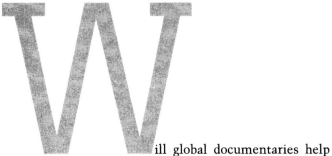ill global documentaries help
us make sense of the world? That is, beyond representing
places and public issues, will they continue to mean anything
at all in a postnational age? Will they report on events in at
least a minimally coherent and objective way? Or will they
move at a speed, and in a fashion, that prevents any significance from being attached to them?

These are open questions, cultural theory notwithstanding. Concerns about the meaning of global television have
been provocative but mostly abstract, based on rather sweep-
ing cultural analyses. Chris Rojek wonders whether "images
of home and abroad, the mundane, order and disorder" might
be "jumbled in a neutral flow of ever-changing images."[1] Kay
Richardson and Ulrike Meinhof ask if a lack of temporal and
spatial grounding might set "viewers loose on a variety of locations bearing no relation to each other or to a starting point."[2]
And Mike Featherstone considers whether viewers can "chain
signifiers into a meaningful narrative" without merely enjoying the "multiphrenic intensities and sensations of the sur-

face of the images."[3] None of these authors believes that global images have entered a state of "free play." But each wonders if borderless communication somehow precludes making sense.

In this chapter, I want to consider these questions in light of what we know about the political economy of documentary television. That is, rather than offering a symptomatic reading of a particular text or zeitgeist (usually based in Europe or North America), I want to focus on transnational patterns of production, distribution, and exchange that might, or might not, produce meaningful documents of the world. I will follow up with a review of the *bête noire* of public service critiques—the American *Survivor* series—and then offer some final thoughts concerning documentary as a form of sensible and significant expression.

Documentary Truth in a Global Age

The question of documentary meaning has never been more complex, given the various epistemological quirks of the transnational marketplace. In contemporary production systems, documentary filmmakers often construct programs without facts, or at least without obvious real-world referents. Footage may be recycled, with some producers reportedly selling images of "Eisenhower-era llamas" to footage-hungry nature programmers around the world.[4] Human subjects may be recycled as well; a British study finds that nearly half of docu-soap participants appear in two or more series.[5] Or footage may be arbitrarily rearranged, with children's science shows offering customized local inserts out of sync with the body of the show. Or, finally, documentary material may be entirely commodified and disconnected from the objects it purportedly represents, as when flora and fauna images from countries like China are sold as generic file footage on world markets.[6] In each case, documentary images seem to be governed less by traditional documentary imperatives—less by a need to record the world and make sense of it—and more by commercial forces for which indexical representation may be an afterthought.

Of course, television documentaries have long been driven by profit as well as pedagogy. Advertising pressures shaped the substance and style of even the most highbrow productions in the public service age.[7] But in a global market, commercial pressures tend to be far more intense and varied, sometimes encouraging producers to rework or disregard traditional notions of representation altogether. In low-budget genres such as children's nature shows, for instance, producers often recycle vault material and concentrate on 3-D effects and animated characters that supposedly make programs attractive to young viewers. Putting animation first and facts second can also generate new revenues as producers create ancillary products from animated characters or use stock footage to lend their programs a sort of generic "universal appeal" (see chapter 3).[8] In these ways and more, commercial pressures often diminish the representational value of documentary programming.

As a result, documentary evidence is often questionable in a global marketplace. Objects or events may be only loosely actual, with cheaper types of travel shows "adapted or even mined for footage which can be used in new shows for international clients."[9] Meanwhile, history shows can use old footage of reenactments or reconstructions—dated clips of battles or Roman ruins, for instance—that are essentially faked twice over, archivally and indexically, and thus doubly removed in time and space from real history.[10] Clearly, commodified documentaries may bear only a loose, "unmotivated" resemblance to the people and subjects they claim to depict.

Global technologies may further remove documentaries from real life. In the most extreme cases, producers use computer-generated pictures to simulate the world's times and places, particularly those lost to view. This is no longer just common practice in low-budget shows. The epic 2000 CBC miniseries *Canada: A People's History*, for instance, used extensive digital effects to conjure up "landscapes of Canada's past."[11] Digital technologies are also used in high-end productions to enhance or rework old photos, using pans, zooms, or even motion simulations that make "the past come to life."[12] In the same way, new exhibition technologies allow producers to "shake off the dust" to make old footage more appealing, colorizing battle reports for a 1999 high-definition television series on World War II, for instance, and including 3-D depictions of tunnels, villages, and landscapes for the *Battlefield* series that was syndicated the same year.[13] Doctored footage may become more commonplace inside and outside traditional broadcast markets as images are digitally compressed and made subject to endless modes of broadcast and online manipulation.

Some observers even insist that documentary viewers have been rewired in a digital age, making today's productions less meaningful at the receiving end. Virtual technologies attract audiences whose "expectations have been informed by very sophisticated computer gaming," a producer says, presumably giving rise to voyeuristic programming that meets (and shapes) demand.[14] Producers may also play with material to attract audiences to new technologies, routinely "massaging" soundtracks to show off the "surround sound" of DVD systems, for instance.[15] In the rush to serve new markets, global producers could conceivably replace real-life images with virtual models, resulting in the "hyperrealization" of documentary filmmaking.

Documentary Genres in a Global Age

But it is not just that producers and viewers are playing fast and loose with the facts. Many producers have stopped making sense of those facts as well by neglecting to place them within conventional narrative structures. Indeed, fact and fiction distinctions have been brazenly brushed aside in a number of markets, though in different ways and to varying degrees. *Television Business International* has noted a worldwide shift toward documentaries that cross the line between history, science, and culture.[16] Meanwhile, "shockumentaries" and other hybrids have swept North and South American markets, like the Canadian specialty channel series that offers a "documentary, comedy, and cooking" format.[17] In the United States, reality sitcoms like *The Osbournes* have become hits on cable and network television. And around the world, superchannels offer new infotainment genres like "kids' science," which features fictional animated characters and a sort of generic mishmash the Discovery Channel describes as "storytelling that has embedded content but isn't 100% factual."[18]

The most notorious generic mix, of course, is the docusoap, or "reality program," as it is known in the United States, which can trace its roots back to entertainment-oriented cop shows and public access programming of the 1960s and 1970s (see chapter 3). Textually, docusoaps are a hybrid and by some accounts a muddle. They offer "facts," but usually of a private and subjective sort. They document the world, but in a melodramatic way closer to entertainment than public affairs program styles. And they show us "real life," but usually as it unfolds on a contrived set where traditional "as found" principles often go by the board. Even the viewing of the shows is hard to pin down as fact or fiction. Increasingly personal and intimate depictions such as the zoom close-ups and elaborate microphone set ups of the *Big Brother* series may appeal less to our desire to know the world than to a sort of idle and irresponsible desire to experience it, vicariously or otherwise—to a sort of voyeuristic or narcissistic need to be near (or in) the action, however sordid or banal. In all these ways, reality shows can no longer be easily categorized as "discourses of sobriety" marked off from fiction or plain old entertainment.

Clearly, global producers mix up what were once relatively distinct modes of representation. But why the mix? And how specifically is genre mixing related to globalization? A number of factors are involved here, many of them more grounded and economic in nature than the broader cultural shifts identified in textually based accounts. A deregulated television market allows for the employment of casualized labor within flexible organizational structures and thus crossovers from fictional to factual programming and vice versa. One producer notes that in a free labor market there are "more people making documentaries who aren't documentarians" and who "could well be making America's Funniest Home Videos."[19] More flexible modes of investment also encourage new forms of collaboration between fictional and factual programmers; "rockumentaries," for instance, allow VH1 to offer a well-rounded brand product, and cross-platformed projects by ABC and Court-TV in the United States allow parent Disney Corporation to promote its output on a number of channels. Genre mixes also offer new revenues for independent producers, as "documercials" yield promotional fees from a number of sources, including Hollywood studios seeking documentary tag-ons for their fictional DVD releases or computer manufacturers who hope the genre will do for information technology "what MTV did for music."[20]

In short, there are myriad reasons—both material and discursive—for documentary hybridity. Market processes work together with emerging technologies, production practices, and broader cultural dynamics to produce new documentary practices and protocols. In some cases, programs are designed to promote products rather than inform viewers. In others, documentary content is generated by subjects or sponsors themselves with little substantive input from filmmakers— a reversal of documentary practice as it has been carried out around the world and over time. In all these ways, documentary seems to have distanced itself from the practical, aesthetic, and epistemological foundations on which the genre was built. In today's spin-off market, a cultural watershed seems to have been crossed.

Documentary Quality in a Global Age

By some accounts, conventional notions of documentary quality and taste have also gone by the board, though again we

should be careful not to exaggerate. Even in an age of corporate diversification, for instance, producers and programmers
make quite extensive efforts to distinguish different types of
cultural products, often upholding traditional hierarchies of
value along the way. The company that makes many of A&E's
blue-chip documentary biographies does not publicize its association with the syndicated show *Third Date* (which chronicles
the lead-up but not the denouement of a couple's first sexual
encounter). Nor do blue-chip producers like to be associated
with reality television for fear that "all documentary programmers [will be] tarred with the same brush."[21] For commercial
as well as cultural reasons, highbrow and lowbrow mixing may
have reached its limits in documentary programming, at least
for the moment.

But there are competing pressures. The dumbing down—or
at least the branching out—of documentary television creates
market opportunities as well as risks and may thus continue as
a trend in the documentary industry. Documentary audiences
may be merged into hybrid infotainment groupings, thereby
generating new revenue possibilities. DNI's *Rough Science*,
for example, is meant to appeal to traditional science viewers
along with a new group of "adventure lovers" who will want to
see a group of researchers put in "survivor mode" and "discover
their way off an island."[22] Other broadcasters may try to keep
highbrow and lowbrow fare to separate parts of the schedule,
though still too close for comfort for some public service critics. The U.K. advocacy group Campaign for Quality Television
contends that the ITV network's "worldwide reputation for
producing major documentaries is coming apart at the seams"
because of its inclusion of prime-time docusoaps that appeal
to crossover audiences.[23] In either case, traditional cultural distinctions may disappear as programmers blend products to create new markets.

Again, the epitome of meaningless and dumbed-down documentaries is the reality shows, which for many critics symbolize not just commercialization but a broader cultural malaise.
Certainly, most of these programs are produced for straight

market reasons. Many are low-budget, produced at a fraction of the cost of other factual fare. Most are low-risk, employing casualized labor rather than the strike-prone unionized crews associated with fiction TV. And virtually all are at least globally "bankable," tackling generic topics and types, mostly in the form of human-interest stories, which are seen to appeal to diverse markets and cultures around the world.

Commercially, the shows seem to make sense. Culturally, however, the case for reality TV is more tenuous. When Russian viewers see a show like *Road Patrol* (which documents highway accidents around Moscow), "they can think there but for fate go I," according to sociologist Igor Kafanilov.[24] When Americans watch cop shows, they want to see "their neighbors up shit creek," according to communications researcher Mary-Beth Oliver.[25] And when British audiences watch docusoaps, they seek visual stimulation "unencumbered by moral or social judgments," according to film studies critic Elizabeth Cowie.[26] The consensus seems to be that docusoaps preclude either real aesthetic experiences or responsible social commitments. They are indefensible, that is, as art or information. This is television that "attacks human dignity," according to the Vatican, a view that has been supported by authorities as diverse as France's main broadcast regulator and the Russian Orthodox Church.[27] It is "programming for numbskulls," according to producer Nick Broomfield.[28] Degenerate strain or sign of things to come, reality programming is widely seen as an assault on both sense and sensibility in broadcast cultures around the world.

Documentary Lineups in a Global Age

If documentaries are produced and distributed in increasingly meaningless ways, what happens to them when they are served up for home viewing? There is at least some reason to believe that meaninglessness—or at least disorderly representation—is compounded at the exhibition stage. Here documentary texts are often sliced and diced to fit broadcast schedules or the perceived tastes of target markets.

Textual coherency may be undermined as programs are grouped together into commercially convenient, rapid-fire, catch-all lineups. According to one producer, schedules structurally contradict documentary meaning, either imposing strict time limits on shows and thus leaving no room for real investigation or jumbling them up together, making context and coherence impossible to sustain.[29] These tendencies could be accentuated in a transnational marketplace where audio-visual products consumed in a number of forms and in a variety of ways become less coherent than they were in the "one product, one audience" age.

Even stable and sensible domestic services may disregard the symbolic structures and hierarchies of earlier eras. Canada's History Television offers a nightly information-entertainment package of documentary features, fictional films, and reality programs designed to contribute to a sort of nightly "historical experience." To be sure, the History Television lineup may make sense but in a rather amorphous way, as a sort of one-stop culture-shopping extravaganza. Here the past may serve as a sort of generic source of pleasure or distraction, but it hardly survives as a carefully organized, historically specific body of knowledge.

Documentaries may make even less sense as they are jumbled together by viewers at home. It seems reasonable to believe that global viewers will zap their remote controls and station-hop programs to create their own "documentary-slash-whatever" texts in a multichannel age, thereby undermining whatever semantic unity the programs had in the first place. In even worse-case scenarios, media-saturated fans may be unable to recognize documentary facts when they see them, with American research suggesting that younger viewers are no longer able to distinguish between fact and fiction in even the schlockiest shows.[30] With these considerations in mind, one might argue that global documentaries have stopped making sense—at every stage of production, in every known market, and in every sense of the word.

Documentary Meaning and Global Audiences

Compelling and disconcerting as these arguments are, some questions remain. Take the meaningless audience critique, for instance: There is actually a good deal of evidence to suggest that documentaries are consumed as meaningful products, in a number of ways, on a routine basis, and in most parts of the world. While information concerning documentary audiences is scarce, survey data suggest that they are perhaps more sedentary and selective—and at least in this way more "sensible"—than other types of viewers. One study of the European ARTE channel argues that documentary television still makes sense even if sense-making requires more work from viewers faced with a quicker mix of times, spaces, and modes of address.[31] Even fans of reality shows—those presumably most caught up in the surface intensities of documentary images —seem to make sense of programs in a more careful and reflexive way than some accounts suggest. One recent ethnographic study of U.K. reality viewers concludes that a "substantial number . . . are extremely skeptical about how many of the real life situations are set up."[32] Many testimonials indicate similar degrees of scrutiny and second-guessing. A recent letter from a Canadian viewer of the *Survivor* series, for instance, reminds us that even "hooked" fans may see through "preening contestants" and "hokey camerawork" while enjoying the show.[33] Similarly, the Websites surrounding *Big Brother* are rife with "split belief" accounts, that is, testimonials from viewers both "caught up" and "ticked off" with reality antics.[34] If anything, existing audience data reveal a widespread concern with the politics of global representation, quite at odds with stereotypes of the viewer-voyeur.

In a similar way, documentary subjects may be more reflexive and sensible than some critiques suggest. Many reality show contestants seem to take into account the personal ramifications of their appearances, as research in the United Kingdom and Norway suggests that most participation takes place on the basis of "informed consent" that suits lifestyle choices. It is also worth noting that a substantial number of viewers stubbornly decline to take part in the reality project: a recent Canadian-U.S. poll suggests a fixed 90 percent "opting out" (across most demographics) because of a fear of public ridicule.[35]

Of course, this does not mean that media-savvy participants no longer need protection from unsavory filmmakers. Exploitation is endemic in the factual television business, where contracts between producers and subjects can be complex, irrevocable, and designed to suit corporate interests. But there is evidence from around the world that audiences and participants are taking an increasingly critical stance toward the industry and its practices. Even topic recycling—for many critics the ultimate sign of commodification and cultural exhaustion —may be a sign of reflexivity on the part of reality subjects. Australian producers note an increasing number of would-be participants withholding informed consent, forcing them to return to familiar sources and issues.[36] In short, documentary subjects may in some circumstances be more knowledgeable about the conditions and consequences of documentary programming. As a result, they may be more inclined to intervene in the production and circulation of factual images— more ready, that is, to act as documentary agents in their own right.

It is also quite possible that audiences make aesthetic and moral judgments concerning the programs they watch, though again we can only deduce this from scattered testimonials. One Canadian viewer defends the American reality series *Chains of Love* as "television's equivalent of Chaucer and the morality tale," and critic John Doyle responds that he has a right to assess the show as a form of "critical filtering."[37] This exchange suggests that documentary may still be judged according to a hierarchy of tastes, albeit a hierarchy more open to challenge than in the public service past, when shows like this might have been dismissed without populist apologies. Further, taste judgments seem to be made in the various discussion groups that now attach themselves to the genre. *Temptation Island* chat rooms may be less disciplined and pedagogically inclined than the public service (educator-led) listener and viewer groups that came before them in the 1940s and 1950s, but they also tend to be more globally reflexive, taking fuller account of the social origins and worldwide repercussions of factual television. A May 2000 bigbrothersux.com panel concerning American "cultural imperialism" is just one case in point. Protests against reality surveillance techniques in Greece, Australia, and France are others. All of these cases suggest that viewers are hardly indifferent to the ethical and epistemological dimensions of documentary filmmaking on a global scale.[38]

It is also worth noting that reality television serves as an important site for the reassertion of national standards of taste around the world, and in a variety of ways. Good television, of course, is usually defined by what it is not, and (foreign) reality programming may serve as a negative example by which (domestic) taste judgments can be made. In Canada, for instance, the reality show *Pioneer Quest* has come to symbolize the superiority or inferiority of homegrown television, with critics and viewers stressing either its "honesty" or "earnest tediousness" compared with its *Survivor* counterpart.[39] *Castaway 2000* and PBS' *Frontier House* have served similar purposes, respectively, for British and American public television fans.[40] Australian critics, for their part, have called attention to the "much more complex narrative structures" of their shows compared with British versions.[41] In short, reality television is not just a space where grounded documentary values are set aside in the name of guilty pleasures. Instead it seems to be an increasingly important site for the assertion of local cultural distinctions, both ethical and aesthetic, and thus the basic elements of documentary meaning. In all these ways, even the

most down-market documentary types may allow and even encourage discriminating, "responsible" viewing.

Documentary Meaning and Global Distribution

Postmodern accounts also tend to disregard distributors and
the ways they work to stabilize documentary meanings and
tastes. Like other service providers, documentary channels try
to maintain a set of product attributes and values that are "coherent, appropriate, distinctive, protectable and appealing to
consumers."[42] In other words, a channel "brands" its product
by offering up a lineup with a clear-cut identity and tone. This
is not to say there are no program surprises. Indeed, finding
a balance between the novel and the predictable is seen as
the key to a successful service; some web distributors promise to "fling the doors wide open" to new types of product.[43]
But established channels like Discovery, the world's third most
successful brand, according to a recent widely published market survey, generally prefer to "err on the side of caution" and
live up to the viewer expectations they have built over time.[44]
In fact, the need to develop an overall product identity or
meaning may be particularly urgent in the competitive world
where existing channels seem to be reemphasizing an identifiable "style and world view," as one programmer puts it, to
distinguish themselves from their competitors.[45] In these circumstances, "meaningful" context may be a way to stand out
from the pack in a multichannel market.

The imposition of "corporate meaning"—of a predictable
symbolic universe—on documentary programs is also a common practice at the commissioning stage. Errol Morris is not
the first producer to be told to include no more than 5 percent new ideas in his work. Indeed, what we know about documentary program buyers suggests that they seek out the tried
more than the new in their lineups, material that "jumps out,"
to be sure, but from more or less established symbolic hori-
zons. CNN's Jennifer Hyde, for one, seeks documentaries of

a similar length and style, all united by their "relevancy to
what is going on in the world" (according to CNN).[46] A&E's
Amy Briamonte seeks immediately clear themes: "maximum
five-liners which jump out at you from the TV Guide."[47]
"Super-programmers" thus seem to be constructing a number
of theme-based markets in which anything emphatically does
not go. On the major documentary channels, commissioning
editors prefer stories that fit a formula and that can thus be
positioned and "made sense" of within a larger text, be it a
series or the channel lineup as a whole. A free play of documentary images is thus rather implausible when one takes
channeling processes into account.

Scheduling works against textual chaos as well, by cluster-
ing programs into more or less coherent blocks where predictable audience flows can take place. The most obvious attempt to discipline viewers in this way is the "theme night,"
an increasingly popular feature of documentary programming
in which similar shows are placed together as part of a concep-
tually coherent prime-time package. Media theorist John Ellis
considers scheduling to be "nothing other than editing on an
Olympian scale,"[48] and the basic principles at work in documentary programming are indeed much like those of a narrative construction. According to programmers at ZDF.doku,
the German documentary digital channel, theme nights "ease
viewers' orientation" to new material. For French and German programmers at the ARTE channel, they offer a series
of "microcosms through which more complex questions can
be understood."[49] And for officials at the Discovery Channel,
they are the sites where "programs come into their own as
concepts."[50]

Of course, only so many documentary meanings and tastes
can be constructed from above, whether by scheduling or other
means. Peter Bazalgette of Endemol UK is probably right when
he says "the days where you can stick [a traditional documentary about foreign affairs] with a popular show on either side
of it . . . are gone"—if only because viewers have so many more
viewing options than they did in the public service age.[51] More-

over, even if audiences can be steered toward worthy shows, they may well enjoy them as "trivialities" or "informational escapism."[52]

But just as clearly, programmers employ a variety of devices to maintain more or less disciplined audience groups and orderly consumption practices, aided and abetted by a variety of new media services. The U.S.-based Documall service, for instance, offers its clients customized schedules in which shows are categorized according to style and theme, backed up by in-depth reviews and search engines to help viewers understand the material.[53] Similarly, in Canada the Internet is used to regulate audience flows and shape viewing experiences with documentary Websites "interlacing show with show, and series with series to draw the audience from place to place within the network brand," according to consultant Tom Johnson.[54] There are thus a number of efforts to channel documentary images and audiences in orderly ways, and it is indeed possible that viewers will be less inclined to mix and match texts there with impunity. All in all, the free play of documentary meaning may be kept in check by market forces much as it was by policy regulation during the public service age.

Documentary Meaning and Global Production

There is also little evidence that producers themselves have abandoned notions of facticity, taste, and meaning in a new documentary age. First, the idea that producers are recycling footage and somehow undermining documentary's indexical ground is questionable, at least as a global assertion. Just as digital archive techniques allow images to be "dredged up," they also encourage producers to pay more attention to the temporal and spatial origins of those images. History producers note that contemporary search engines make "generic placement" increasingly unacceptable,[55] and they point to a backlash against the "plumbing of the vaults."[56] We should also keep in mind recent injunctions by the Australian Broadcasting Corporation and other networks that require that file footage "be clearly identified as such on screen, when not to do so would confuse or mislead the viewer."[57] If anything, factual sounds and images seem to be more indexically grounded than ever, especially when one considers the sorts of simulations and reenactments that were commonplace in the public service era.[58]

Second, there is little evidence that documentarists have cut their special indexical ties to the world. Relatively few filmmakers create sights and sounds from scratch without regard to real-world referents. Indeed, facticity seems to be more strictly enforced than ever by organizations as far-flung as the U.S. Federal Communications Commission with respect to fraud in American reality shows,[59] the U.K.'s Independent Television Commission with regard to "breach of trust" in British docusoaps,[60] and the Australian Broadcasting Corporation with respect to "checkbook journalism" in public affairs programming.[61] In all these cases, the world's broadcast authorities have tried to maintain the as-found integrity of documentary material. Recent reprimands in France and even a jail term for a German producer suggest that standards of documentary truth continue to be enforced in factual markets around the world.[62]

Factual distinctions may also be sustained in more controversial infotainment forms. Take factual reenactments, for instance. The charge is often made that the "line between [historical documentary and docudrama] has become increasingly blurred" as producers use more "elaborate and aggressive re-creation techniques borrowed from fiction as well as factual films."[63] In fact, the way these shows are actually produced suggests an altogether more nuanced practice with its own technical and aesthetic techniques. Most re-creations avoid personalized depictions and full frontal shots, and many others take advantage of relaxed union rules to employ amateur "re-enactors" rather than actors.[64] In short, reenactments usually look different than straight fact or fiction, and few would be confused with documentaries or dramas by viewers even roughly familiar with the basic lexicons of contemporary television. In fact, Canadian research suggests that audiences are easily able to distinguish between file footage and re-creations, while generally finding the latter less convincing if more fun to watch.[65] In case there is any doubt, re-creations are often explicitly labeled as such, especially in more controversial point-of-view programs. At the Australian Broadcasting Corporation, news and current affairs re-creations are used only in "exceptional cases" and "must be clearly identified as such and presented in a way that will not mislead the audience."[66]

Also more than ever, producers seem to be ensuring that re-creations are factually grounded to some degree. In the United Kingdom, companies like Cromwell Productions routinely check their scripts with historical experts like the Royal Military Academy. In the United States, the PBS series *American Experience* hires two or three academic advisors for each show who act as "lawyers to keep us from getting in trouble," according to the executive producer.[67] And in Canada, broadcasters like History Television only allow reenactments if words are pulled verbatim from a historical record.[68] None of this is to deny that the lines between fact and fiction in documentary programming have been redrawn, sometimes in a more liberal direction. But it is to clearly challenge the idea of a universal, progressive blurring of information and entertainment. Re-creations are certainly mutable and sometimes unpredictable as modes of representation, but they hardly entail an implosion of fact and fiction.

Truth claims made for reenactments further suggest that facticity is not so much dead as different in documentary production today. True, reenactments are sometimes offered up as "hyperrealities," more actual than file footage per se. Producer Michael Resnick says his World War I reenactments represent field strategy better than any actual archive material, which was almost all reenacted in the first place. He insists that restaged battles take place in a "perfectly controlled environment [that] reveal[s] the underlying patterns" of the war.[69]

But more often, reenactments are considered a second-best to actuality. Many European and American program buyers demand that reenactments comprise less than half of a program.[70] Canadian critics, for their part, regard reenactments as separate and unequal types of documentary evidence; John Doyle calls them "gimmicks with a grain of truth" that should never be allowed to replace history per se.[71] In short, even the best reenactments seem to be widely regarded as a sort of quasirealism that reveals traces of the past but falls short of being a "document." In most markets, reenactments are defended as provisional evidence within a hierarchical set of truths.

The way images are digitally generated suggests that facts are still taken seriously in a global documentary age. Digital manipulation can be taken as plain proof that traditional efforts to record the world have been displaced by a more ambitious project to create facts from scratch. But a number of epistemological controversies around the world suggest otherwise. Take, for instance, the recent colorization of images of World War II, the generation of images of *World War III*, and the wholesale reconstruction of prehistoric life for natural-history documentaries. All indicate that program makers are less indifferent than reflexive when it comes to factual questions—questions that continue to be hotly debated and frequently resolved by producers themselves. The European makers of a colorized documentary on World War II, for instance, say they thought "long and hard about the ethical and moral issues" before concluding that the material would have been shot in color had the technology been available at the time.[72] The producers of *World War III* argued that they were showing "how subjective documentaries are" at the best of times, an argument accepted by few broadcasters other than Italy's RAI3 and Germany's ZDF, which aired the program in 1999.[73] And the makers of the 1995 BBC production *Walking with Dinosaurs* say their animatronic images were at least iconically true, based on a sort of testable speculation.[74] In all these cases, new technologies helped change the rules con-

cerning documentary facts, but they hardly made those rules—
and the meanings associated with them—irrelevant.[75]

All in all then, there is a good deal of evidence to suggest
that global documentaries will make sense as facts for viewers,
albeit differently than they did in the public service past. But
to get a better sense of the state of factual meaning in documentary television, we should again consider the programs
themselves. Perhaps a last look at what has been a particularly
controversial type—the nature show—will help us determine
more precisely how documentaries "document" in a global age.

An Example: Let's Do It Like We Did
in the Discovery Channel

For most critics, nature shows epitomize the "meaninglessness" of postmodern, postnational television. Many offer a collage of sights and sounds with no obvious real-world objects of
representation and no apparent pedagogical purpose. Animal
Planet promises its viewers "all animals, all the time," that is,
a disparate, mostly decontextualized set of images united only
by what the channel calls a "love of critters."[76] Market conditions may well encourage programmers to recycle flora and
fauna as often as they please; indeed many of the shows are
aimed at younger viewers presumably unfamiliar with image
archives and the protocols of indexing.[77] But the practice is not
found in crass commercial circles alone. Even conscientious
blue-chip producers like the BBC's Natural History Unit keep
animal sounds dating back to 1946 for future use as "atmosphere."[78] In cases like these, footage seems to be devoid of ref-
erential let alone instructional value.

There are other ways in which nature shows no longer make
sense in a strict documentary way. Nature sounds, for instance, are rarely "real," if only because most animals do not
make interesting noises, and those that do are hard to record
over the whir of a camera. Most production contracts require
operators to record just twenty minutes of "clean atmosphere"

sound a day for a small part of a shoot; this material then is supplemented by a variety of computerized effects and archived "ambiance."[79] Most nature sounds are thus "actual" in a metonymic sense at best, with individual noises representing the entire repertoire of a species rather than a particular animal on screen (that is, assuming they are not simulated entirely). From an audio point of view, then, nature television's documentary status is decidedly shaky, with programs engaged less in a straight act of reference than a sort of stylistic free play.

Further, even these tenuously "real-life" sounds and images are assembled within loosely defined generic categories in which distinctions between fact and fiction are increasingly unclear. Children's nature shows frequently rely on animated characters to tell their stories because they are entertaining, because they have a wider international appeal than real-life hosts, and because they don't have to be paid. And with producers spending more on nature characters, they often have less money for actual documentary images, forcing them to go to the "vaults" for cheap stock footage, which comes to represent nature in a general sense. In these ways, nature shows seem to have crossed all boundaries—historical, geographic, and symbolic—with impunity.

Notions of quality and taste also seem to have gone by the board. A growing number of programs adhere to the American "feed, fuck, and kill" formula.[80] Indeed, the dumbing down of global nature television could well gain momentum as new players with questionable commitments to public service modes of representation enter the field. In some areas, cut-throat corporate competitors such as Rupert Murdoch's News Corporation are taking over nature superchannels such as the National Geographic Network. At the same time, producers who are not documentarists by training are entering the business for largely commercial reasons.[81] In these new market conditions, nature programming may offer placeless and pointless programming.

Finally, nature fans seem to be less concerned with facts and meaning per se. Though hardly proof in itself, the 2000 pop music hit "Let's Do It Like We Did on the Discovery Channel" suggests enough viewers are tuning in for prurient rather than pedagogical reasons to make a hook for a well-known song. Indeed, nature programs may be designed to discourage serious viewing altogether, with increasingly intimate (and intrusive) filming techniques appealing less to a desire to know the world than to the pleasures derived from mastering, controlling, and consuming its images. In this sense, nature shows seem closer to pornography than documentary. Wildlife voyeurism seems to be a long-term trend grounded in well-established production practices dating back to the public service era and before. The melodramatic strategies of early filmmakers like Robert Flaherty are by now well known to cinema students. Less notorious is the video voyeurism of public service broadcasters, including the BBC's first infrared close-ups of bird nests in 1955, its first color broadcasts in the late 1960s, and its experiments in time-lapse microphotography in the 1970s. All of these techniques were meant to deliver an experience as well as a science lesson to audiences.[82] The same can be said for the various "critter cams" developed by nature programmers in the following decades that allowed viewers to "eavesdrop on the hidden world of animals."[83] Clearly the genre has come a long way from the days when visuals in some quarters at least were designed for "illustrative" purposes only—a time when color photography was seen to be a distraction even at commercial enterprises like National Geographic Magazine.[84] In nature programs, spectacle and sensationalism seem to have slowly but surely taken precedence over information and meaning.

It is easy to dismiss these charges as we did above with regard to other types of factual programming. After all, new technologies and markets may encourage producers to represent actual animals in more or less orderly ways. Digitalization makes footage more accessible than ever and has apparently made animal simulations less acceptable than in the past.[85] Further, filmmakers may realize they can only "recycle so many sexy predators a year" in an image-saturated market without everyone—producers and viewers included—collapsing in a state of cultural exhaustion.[86] Finally, distributors may continue to help viewers make sense of "actual" documentary material in predictable ways, if only to assist their own corporate branding efforts. An Animal Planet official notes, "We're not just a network that shows a series of unrelated documentaries—there is an editorial spine behind all of this that weaves together in a way people will find entertaining and fun."[87]

But all the same, one can argue that nature shows no longer "mean" what they did in a national public service age. Indexical or not, documentary data seem to be constituted quite differently in today's markets and in ways that alter the meaning and significance of the programs themselves. The Discovery Channel's "facts," for instance, are often derived from events sponsored and created by the channel itself, such as the exploration of the Titanic or the raising of a frozen mammoth in Siberia; and though this material is presumably accurate as far as it goes, it can hardly be taken as independent "truth." Of course, contrived evidence has been a staple of nature documentaries since Flaherty's first "Eskimo" films. But what is new is that contrivedness now seems to be an intrinsic part of the Discovery documentary's appeal and a parcel of its meaning, at least as far as programmers are concerned. Discovery Channel officials want its programs to be understood and appreciated as staged documentary events, as one official notes: "Consumers know that we document these sorts of things, but they also need to understand that we're out there making them happen."[88] Making viewers understand the role of Discovery in the creation of documentary truth is now an explicit part of the documentary experience rather than a secret or a "reality" one must disavow to enjoy the program. As nature programs become "events," and a part of what they were once meant to be about, documentary truth is arguably more provisional than it once was. The archetype of the mediated event and perhaps the epitome of the blurring of reality and representation in nature programming is the Discovery Tour, introduced as one of the channel's ancillary products in the 1990s, during which tourists' real-life adventures are meant to match what they saw on TV.

One might argue also that global nature programs are no longer meant to mean something in a purely factual sense. Catherine Lamour of Canal Plus says "viewers want meaning, but they also want . . . to be moved, to be inside a story."[89] Many producers similarly welcome DVDs not as informational technologies but as improved sensual packages that give a heightened sense of proximity to a documentary event. In this view, documentaries appeal not so much to viewers' sense of epistophelia, to their desire to know, but to their desire to feel, a need that documentaries can meet precisely because they are factual and thus more emotionally "moving" or resonant than fiction alone. Documentaries, by this account, continue to mean something (indeed indispensably so), but as a means to bring viewers somewhere else altogether—to a sensual and affective rather than a purely cognitive realm. It is precisely this new sensual-cognitive experience that nature channels seem to be selling, with many services selecting topics as much for their digital spin-off potential as for their intrinsic truth or significance.[90] Again, the point is not that nature channels are devoid of facts, but that these seem to be of far more instrumental value than they once were. In this sense, the status of meaning, like the status of place and public discussion, may have changed profoundly on global television.

Another Example: *Survivor Marquesas*

But putting aside producer designs or audience responses, what can we say about factual texts themselves as meaningful documents? Do global programs still make credible and coherent truth claims? And, in doing so, do they help viewers act within and upon their worlds? In this section, I want to take a closer look at the *bête noire* of public service criticism: the reality series *Survivor*, a European reality format adapted for the

American market in 2000 that has since come to symbolize all the fakeness and banality of documentary in a global era.

As a meaningless "reality" experience, *Survivor* seems to have it all. The series documents the world, but only in the kitschiest and most superficial of ways. *Survivor*'s world is essentially an exotic backdrop or playground for increasingly contrived actuality sets. *Survivor* stereotypes its locales, with Africa for instance serving as a "location inhabited by malaria-bearing insects and dangerous predators."[91] Or it physically reconstructs them, as with Pulau Tiga, the Malaysian setting for *Survivor I* built from scratch, based on what executive producer Mark Burnett calls ideas from "cultural anthropology, religious ritual and Robert Louis Stevenson."[92]

It is particularly in this second respect that the show's empirical grounding is suspect. For instance, *Survivor I* producers built a "local bar" and shipped in "natives" so that contestant Kelly Wigglesworth could be seen enjoying the "only authentically 'Malaysian' night of her trip"—she "would have needed a global positioning system to know where she was," boasted Burnett—and so presumably would viewers. As it turned out, Wigglesworth's "local" excursion simply took her to the other side of the island, still well within the boundaries of her prefab playground.[93] It is worth noting here that "real" Malaysians were almost totally excluded from *Survivor*'s Malaysian setting—a job made easier because this area had been uninhabited since it was created by a volcanic eruption in 1899. *Survivor*'s first island was just the sort of indexical blank slate producers were looking for. Indeed, more settled locations like Australia's Queensland coast (the setting of *Survivor II*) and Kenya's Shaba game reserve (the setting of *Survivor III*) proved much less amenable to stage management. In each case and in shows that followed, elaborate security measures were required to keep local "intruders" at bay.

In a similar way, *Survivor*'s settings were the result of a sort of hyperreal reshaping. *Survivor I*'s tribal council setting, for instance, was a sort of generic pastiche of "faux Mayan columns surrounded by a [South Pacific style] communal fire lava pit."[94] *Survivor II* settled for a "combination of Stonehenge-like rock structures and Aboriginal symbolism that [would flow] with the surroundings,"[95] though the show's art director was instructed to give councils and challenge sites an "indigenous feel" that never descended into "parody."[96] Even the dating of the show was unclear, as filming was time-shifted but presented as a live-to-broadcast text. Finally, topical references were edited out of the text and the results of the competitions kept secret until months after the final vote (followed by a live reunion of contestants). In every way, times and spaces were meant to be "evocative," "transforming the armchair adventurer into the realm of fantasy." Burnett writes that "no suggestion of the real world [was to be] allowed."[97] If anything, the world's places served as free-floating signifiers for *Survivor*'s increasingly fantastic story lines. "The mountains, the desert, the jungles, the beaches," enthuses Burnett with reference to his Australian location. "I wanted it all."[98]

Not only are *Survivor*'s real-life referents unclear—they are presented in both fictional and factual ways. At times the show's status as actuality or entertainment seems to be deliberately fudged, for largely practical reasons. CBS, the host American network, has had a hard time developing the show because production adheres to tight entertainment-type schedules while dispensing with easily controlled stage sets (other than the tribal council). As a production, *Survivor* remains an uneasy melange of fact and fiction.[99] The show's "personality-host," Jeff Probst, is a generic mix, a former VJ whose job it is to maintain a "fine line between reality and scripted makeover."[100] The executive producer is a former marketer who set up Eco-Challenge overland endurance races before getting the idea of documenting them for fans who could not attend. And the contester-subjects themselves tend to take the role of fictional characters, including parts from the old American sitcom *Gilligan's Island*.[101] All of these participants work within the confines of what producers call a "dramality" show,[102] carefully stocked with character types and packaged into highly predictable three-act story structures consisting of "arrival," "friction," and "victory" segments. According to the show's creator, Mark Burnett, the whole concept is "Melrose Place meets Eco-Challenge."[103]

Survivor can make a claim to be "actual," but only if we stretch the meaning of that term. True, the show does present itself as a carefully constructed snapshot of "life today" and the struggle for survival in the "real" world. Staging and manipulation are seen to be quite compatible with this sort of "reality," actually helping the show reveal bigger social truths. "That [the tribal council] had been constructed in a jungle and that TV cameras and lighting surrounded it did not make [it] any less real," Burnett has insisted. "Reality" here stems from the "brutal unscripted truth" the set was designed to yield on a routine basis.[104] *Survivor* can be seen as finely tuned reality apparatus—a demographically balanced, environmentally controlled machine that can "make things happen" for all to see, revealing secrets about individuals and society in the process. "If ever a device were invented to help men and women gauge the caliber of their characters, *Survivor* is it," claims Burnett.[105] In these ways, *Survivor* is the quintessential hyperfactual text —a model of society more real than society itself, which for some critics calls the state of the original into question.[106]

And just as the real is provisional in *Survivor*, it tends to be utterly banal. The show has come to epitomize dumbed-down factual television for many critics, offering bland portraits of formula personalities grandstanding in the name of greed. This is television lacking all depth and "distinction" in academic terms. As a contest *Survivor* is a low-class "game of participation," as Bourdieu might call it,[107] based mostly on luck and the promise of a big payoff (US$1 million for the winner, US$100,000 for the runner-up). As a text, *Survivor* is the antithesis of the sublime, offering up melodramatic story lines pumped up with every sort of musical and visual gimmick. And as a home entertainment product, *Survivor* is tried-and-true escapism offering viewers the sort of "high-octane thrills" they once got from game shows and now look for at the factual end of the schedule. In every way, *Survivor*'s meaning and value is disputable.

Survivor IV: Marquesas is true to form in all respects. Broadcast in the spring of 2002, the first show begins with an aerial shot of a boat accompanied by a world music soundtrack of tribal voices, flutes, and bongo drums. "We're onboard the fishing trawler Amaryllis, making our way through the rough waters of the South Pacific," explains host Jeff Probst from on deck. "Down below, deep inside the hold, are sixteen Americans about to be abandoned in the middle of Tahiti's mystical islands, thousands of miles from the world's nearest continent." This episode will be "realer than ever," Probst insists, as contestants now are required to forage for their own food and necessities "using the resources of the land and their own survival skills." It is the "ultimate challenge, forced to work together to create a new society while battling the elements and each other." Probst declares, "Thirty-nine days, sixteen people, one survivor," and introduces the first episode of the show.

The program begins with contestants jumping into the water, swimming to their team canoes, and paddling to shore. Immediately, personality types and conflicts emerge. "We were singing and trying to get some kind of motion. It really brought us together," explains Gabriel in the first of the show's many off-set asides (though when a *Survivor* character is really off-set is unclear). "My first thought when we hit the beach was 'Thank you, God,'" exclaims Sean, the born-again Christian African American, who insists that everybody was helping out except Sara, the self-described "babe" of the show. Her arrival was "like Cleopatra, like the servants were paddling, and she's sitting on a crate with her boobs hanging out and her goldilocks in the air." Sean explicitly raises the issue of race when he notes that he's from Harlem and wants "to be representing." The importance of gender in the show is also underlined, as Patty, an African-American health worker from Seattle, observes that Sara has a "very cute body . . . and if you have it, of course, use it . . . if she connects with the right individual that may help her get through this."

The rest of the segment is taken up with the search for food and water and preparations for an "immunity challenge" in which the losing team will have to vote one of its members off the island. Again, demographics figure prominently in this part of the show. Patricia, a middle-aged truck assembler from Michigan claims she's in danger of being banished because she is a "woman, old, overweight, and they think I'm a mom figure." Sara plans to vote off Peter, the island's self-styled "mystic" because he's got a "weird look on his face and he just doesn't fit in." Sean is gunning for Sara, who is shown drifting in the lagoon—"other than having two floating devices and looking cute, how can she help us out?" he asks. "It's not chauvinistic, but the more males you have in a camp, the better you can survive."

The show concludes with a tribal council meeting in which each contestant lights a torch that will be snuffed out if he or she is voted off. "We do this because fire represents life," explains Probst. "All over the Marquesas there are ancient dwellings like this one, thousands of years, all sorts of things have taken place, everything from sacrifices to other rituals." Probst continues with the analogy: *Survivor's* tribal council is "certainly ritual, the vote is definitely a sacrifice, because this is where you're held accountable for your actions on the island—that's what this is all about."

As it turns out, the mystic is the first contestant voted off the island, and after a few direct-to-camera asides from his fellows explaining their vote, the first episode of *Survivor IV* comes to an end. "You've survived the vote," Probst tells those who are left. "Go back and build your world. It's only been three days. Anything can happen. I'll see you tomorrow."[108]

Survivor IV is as meaningful—and meaningless—as its predecessors. The show's time and space referents are unclear from the outset. The opening credits show a set of Maoris and Dayaks dancing to world music, followed by a montage of contestants juxtaposed with "the land"—a generic South Sea island they "will be a part of" for the next few weeks. Moreover, the program never veers from its "dramality" story structure, showing stock characters engaged in elaborate activities within carefully staged sets. *Survivor IV* also offers voyeuristic pleasures rather than worldly illumination. The first episode, like others, features confidential direct-to-viewer asides coupled with a bewildering array of bird's-eye views, pans, zooms, and time-lapse environment shots, all presumably designed to appeal to our desires for narrative one-upmanship and sensual intoxication. Indeed, the first two minutes of *Survivor IV* consist of 142 shots from 103 vantage points.

At the same time, *Survivor IV* hardly dispenses with truth and meaning entirely. The show deliberately engages social issues—at the very least the politics of the personal—at numerous junctures. Gender, race, class, and age issues loom large in the competitions and are obviously seen to add "depth" to the text, where they figure as integral "truths" concerning people and power. In fact, it is the show's "controlled and charged" environment that allows Burnett's "elemental forces" to come to the surface. *Survivor* thus both pursues and disregards the usual social preoccupations of a public service text.

But even if *Survivor* speaks the truth, it does so far more uncertainly than its documentary predecessors. First of all, the show is only contingently actual, based on aggressive producer interventions at every stage of the production, from conception to casting to denouement. This is staged reality, a contrived document, even if arguments about fakery are, as Burnett insists, beside the point. With the show's documentary value entirely dependent upon production management, *Survivor* reminds us how far some global documentaries have come from their as-found principles. *Survivor* shows us not life in an ethnographic sense but events manufactured by offstage handlers. Indeed it boasts of that fact.

Moreover, the meaning of those events seems to be offered up not as an end in itself but as a supplement to personal drama and spectacle. Cultural-contextual details are clearly icing on the cake in the *Survivor* package. Fans who buy the companion book or log onto the official Website may know "more about the [cultural settings] than many of the contestants."[109] And regular viewers may learn something about the AIDS crisis in Africa, the intricacies of Polynesian customs, and the environmental problems of the South China Sea. But judging from the in-show promotions and the viewer testimonials, these are peripheral points of interest at best—options added onto what remains a "depthless" text. It is in these cavalier ways that *Survivor* offers meaning and truth in a global age.

Conclusion

It seems fair to say that global documentaries no longer mean what they did in a public service age. A close look at the markets and texts of factual television suggests that global documentary meaning is increasingly provisional—dispensable and open to challenge—though hardly in the universal and total ways forecast in some accounts. Documentaries still make sense, distinctions are still made between fact and fiction, and these distinctions are still enforced by a number of institutions in a number of places. But meaning as such is governed by new rules and new values in the *Survivor*-Discovery era—offered up as a sort of program by-product or a value-added feature rather than a value in itself. In the next chapter, I want to examine this trend more closely with reference to a specific technology, focusing on the ways documentaries might "document" in a digital era.

SIX

Digital Documentary

In this book, I have argued that documentary has taken a global direction that requires us to rethink it as a genre. I have stressed three overall trends in this regard. First, documentary is no longer a national cinematic form produced first and foremost by the nation-state and its cultural institutions. Second, documentary is no longer a public service genre dedicated to the representation of places and public issues for more or less captive audiences. And finally, documentary is no longer an epistemologically secure project, the truth and meaning of which depend upon special indexical ties to the world. Clearly documentary has changed, and at least some of these changes can be attributed to its position in a global marketplace.

My specific question in this chapter is: what directions might documentary take in a digital age? Will the genre continue to be attached to a particular medium? If not, what new types of production (and pleasure) might it entail? How will documentary's traditional objects of representation evolve? Will places and issues retain their status as objects of representation, or will they somehow give way to "virtual" digital models? Will texts themselves make sense in the semiotic free play of the multichannel marketplace? And finally, will documentaries continue to exist at all, as new distribution platforms allow for more or less instant forms of global communication?

Documentary in the Age of Instant Information

Perhaps we should tackle that last question first, since on it hinge many of the others. Will documentaries survive on television, and if so, will they bear any resemblance to documentaries as we knew them? It is worth noting that there are many skeptics. Producers and pundits often point to the appeal of live information, particularly global live information, in broadcast markets around the world. Nothing brings audiences together like an event, we are told, and events by their definition involve a degree of shared simultaneity. In the case of television, a truly communal ritual is seen to involve audiences watching things happen together in real time, as they unfold—or at the very least watching recorded occurrences at the same time as part of a more or less collective experience. From this point of view, recorded documentaries are decidedly uneventful, if not obsolete. After all, most documentaries are hardly "live" in either sense of the word. And very few are popular, at least in terms of TV ratings and box office ticket sales.

But all of these arguments should be treated with caution. For instance, critics are wrong when they say contemporary television is essentially a live medium, with the Internet serving as a backup (or backwater) of archival material. True, broadcast documentary seems to be profiting from programming that is live in both senses of the word. The Discovery Network's live coverage in 2000 of the raising of the Titanic was billed as a "watch with the world event" and gained the network its second-highest audience numbers ever. At the same time, this sort of programming may have allowed for a degree of global communion and connection unimaginable in a mere "duty documentary." Indeed, the millennial fanfare accorded to the *Titanic* show—seen in more than one hundred countries in twenty languages—is virtually unprecedented for a recorded program of any sort.

But for all that, "liveness" hardly makes documentary obsolete. Rather, in today's information marketplace, documentaries frequently complement as well as compete with live broadcasts. *Titanic*, for instance, was followed by a documentary companion piece that was even more widely viewed, and this has been the case with many other Discovery live features. The lines between documentary and live service are increasingly blurred in specialty lineups of all sorts in today's markets. "Live" broadcasters like CNN often stress the documentary value of their productions and feature investigative reports that provide background on events in the news. At the same time, documentary broadcasters promote their programs as "virtual" live broadcasts, with extensive multimedia promotions leading up to the big day of a viewing event (when we can indeed "watch with the world"). In short, television's temporal modes are no longer mutually exclusive, if they ever were. For this reason alone there will probably be a place for documentaries in all sorts of schedules and for the foreseeable future.

Documentary in the "Post-Televisual" Age

Perhaps the more compelling question is not whether television needs documentary but whether documentary needs television. Will the genre continue to be associated with broadcasting or even narrowcasting media? Will documentary programs continue to be shown on small screens in conventional domestic settings? Indeed, will documentaries continue to be "programs" at all?

The argument that documentary is entering a post-televisual era is plausible, at least on the surface. True, documentary television has survived the digital age so far—indeed,

Time Warner's forecast of an upcoming "Internet century"[1] seems rather farfetched in the wake of the millennial "dot-bomb." But that said, digital online technologies have made inroads in the production and distribution of factual programming that will surely survive market booms and busts. Already, post-broadcasting transmission systems have been embraced by both commercial and cultural wings of the industry. Major documentary channels like Canal Plus and PBS began creating Internet subsidiaries in the late 1990s,[2] while others such as CNN aggressively "converged" their broadcast and online operations. Webcasts have also been introduced to great fanfare at broadcast markets like MIPDOC and cultural festivals like Banff 2000, and they have been hailed as "critical to the future of the documentary."[3] At the same time, an independent online production sector has emerged in which a number of firms offer dedicated web productions in some form or another. In the nature program sector, Discovery has invested more than US$500 million in online service to promote e-commerce and streaming opportunities.[4] And in the reality marketplace, series like *Big Brother* have set up twenty-four-hour Web services that give viewers a peek at "off-air" sets and subjects.[5] Even conventional shows like *Survivor* have become ratings hits with the help of Web promotions.[6]

The Internet may also have become a multipurpose distribution vehicle as more documentary programs are made available online. Canada's U8TV and an Irish counterpart have emerged as the first around-the-clock reality-based TV stations presenting continuous Webcasts of documentary and live material.[7] Producers and programmers seem to have noticed these cross-media successes and planned accordingly. One global survey suggests nearly three-fourths of documentarians take online production into account when developing a project, and some of them frequently include a "cyber-element" in their pitches.[8] Meanwhile, conventional broadcasters such as the BBC say they will no longer "take program pitches without interactive elements such as . . . the internet."[9] Piecemeal as the evidence is, we can safely say that documentaries are no longer attached to a particular medium the way they were in the cinema or broadcast eras.

That said, documentary's days on television are not necessarily numbered. To begin with, there are just too many glaring problems with competing media from a commercial perspective. Revenue is hard to collect from online viewing, for instance, just as distribution deals tend to be more complicated than for a simple broadcast. As for subsidiary products, online stock footage companies and the like have made little money and have been plagued with legal problems.[10] Even the online projects that survive will almost certainly benefit from broadcast investment as a sustainable source of funding in the long term.[11] Finally, documentary Webcasting is problematic because of the faltering demand for broadband service,[12] which has made many new media productions invisible even in developed media markets.

These may be short-term glitches, but there is every reason to believe a converged documentary industry will need television for the foreseeable future. Documentary programmers' ideas about convergence tend to be vague—as one operator notes, "All agree it is coming, but no one agrees what it means."[13] Nonetheless, a core conventional wisdom has emerged that suggests television will survive as a documentary platform though in conjunction with other media. For Discovery, convergence is best seen as a "space between established media,"[14] with television and computers serving as separate but complementary devices that enhance the market value of each. In the CNN scenario, Websites will promote and embellish more or less conventional programs.[15] In BBC forecasts, convergence will give rise to "new forms of [documentary] creativity."[16] Actual investors are more cautious, however, and often belie the rhetoric. BBC, for instance, continues to compartmentalize broadcast and online productions and gives Websites relatively low priority.[17] PBS hopes to develop a full-fledged interactive broadcast-Webcast model but remains "inhibited by the cost of . . . true parallel productions."[18] Even DNI, the most ambitious digital investor, views online ventures as "enhanced TV applications," albeit involving their own production skills, copyright rules, and modes of sponsorship.[19] Meanwhile, National Geographic's online operations have been mostly limited to online video samples of its TV productions.[20]

Clearly, then, no major documentary distributor regards the Internet as a viable stand-alone medium. Mainstream programmers may offer online services like backup trivia platforms or after-the-fact discussion forums, but very little view the Internet as a source of information or entertainment in its own right. If anything, the cyber-sector faces an uncertain future even as an afterthought to broadcasting, as major players like CNN and DNI scale back their services or merge them entirely with television operations.[21] Certainly, "Net doc" problems can be blamed on old media's lack of vision or enthusiasm for new services. Be that as it may, online productions show no sign of replacing television documentaries anytime soon.

Thus, the most likely scenario is some form of enhanced multimedia delivery that will change the way documentaries are produced, put together, and viewed at home or elsewhere. Bigger screens, sharper sounds, and better pictures, for instance, could lead to new program styles—new sorts of sound, images, and graphics packaged into new sorts of factual exposition and storytelling. New recording (and deleting) technologies could in turn lead to unconventional viewing experiences as high-quality, "home-edited" documentaries engage viewers in something more than the casual glance that has traditionally been associated with television.[22] At the same time, interactive technologies could extend and deepen modes of engagement to provide a range of extra-textual and ancillary spaces that recruit documentary audiences as fans rather than as mere take-it-or-leave-it spectators. Documentaries could even enlist viewers as part-time producers who shape texts through voting and other sorts of audience intervention.[23] All of this is possible and certainly worth thinking about. Indeed, the aesthetics and pleasures of digital documentary may require urgent attention and a rethinking of documentary studies in the very near future. But varied as they are, most documentary scenarios involve television. Broadcasting or narrowcasting of some sort will almost certainly be a staple part of documentary in the foreseeable future.

Documentation in a Digital Age

But even if television remains documentary's chief medium, how will documentaries "document" in a digital age? To stick with our earlier questions, how will they represent places and public issues in meaningful ways?

In some respects, the possibilities for local representation in a digital age are unprecedented. The Internet can be seen as a local or "interlocal" medium that allows collectivities to express themselves in new ways while reaching out to like-minded counterparts across the world. Even megaservices like Discovery claim to tailor online networks to the needs of particular "communities."[24] Conventional broadcast networks also promise to make room for online localism, with CNN's *Cold War* series laying the groundwork for what it calls a worldwide "on-line archive system" in which eyewitness accounts get equal space with official versions of historical events.[25] For new media services, the possibilities (if not probabilities) are endless. One observer sees a giant local image bank from which everyone could download sounds and images of his or her hometown. Others say audiences will create self-images from scratch because of falling equipment costs.[26] Even critics who regard television as a "major disaster" for local production hope the Internet will not succumb to the same mistakes.[27] In all these views, digital documentary could serve as a "network of record" for the world's places.

Online documentaries may also allow for new forms of public expression. Digital discussions certainly seem harder to curb than their broadcast counterparts. Derek Paget, for instance, has noted the difficulties corporations like McDonald's have had shutting down online documentary forums in recent "McLibel" cases.[28] At the same time, alternative perspectives may be more accessible than ever as search engines like Documall allow viewers to create their own program packages from scratch without corporate mediation.[29] Meanwhile, new distributors like Amazon.com promise to build virtual "common carrier" networks without corporate filters, giving access to programs that are "more profane and less formulaic" than regular television.[30] Some observers insist this digital wave of ideas is largely unstoppable. New collective modes of production and distribution may make even copyright rules unenforceable.[31]

Finally, digital documentaries promise to make sense of the world in less restrictive ways. For instance, DVD productions may provide a graphic, nonlinear view of the world, richer and more layered than traditional "discourses of sobriety." Programs like these may generate the sparks or at least the visceral responses and flights of imagination so vital to democratic practice and subject formation. At the same time, their online counterparts may allow for new forms of dialogue with the documentary form, undermining authoritative (and authoritarian) modes of communication along the way.[32] At least fledgling examples of these new types of digital meaning are found in public service and even some commercial networks' background sites and discussion platforms as digital documentary services.[33] Even in the heart of the digital marketplace, then, we find spaces where genuine public opinion might take shape.

But there are limits to all this. Most obviously, documentary diversity may be bogged down by stubborn monopolies and the inability of local and "alternative" services to compete with their big-budget counterparts. Lacking finances and brand names, small-scale operators may be shunted off to the margins of mega-distribution networks. This is a problem that could become serious indeed if large networks are allowed to exclude smaller competitors from their own lineups and interactive program guides.[34]

Indeed, the "public sphere" model may be a nonstarter in

postbroadcasting networks as well. "Public spaces" provided by Amazon.com, for instance, will only include productions "that meet the criteria for violence, nudity and production quality."[35] At other services, content guidelines are becoming increasingly evident as well. Meanwhile, few corporate sites allow for robust forms of public response; many conduct instant polling regarding program issues but not much else.

Copyright restrictions could also be stricter in a digital age. One American producer's claims to "fair use" of material from global satellite broadcasts remains unresolved because of the difficulty of determining whether such material is being used for critical commentary or commercial exploitation.[36] Some "alternative" distributors like www.undergroundfilm .com have stopped accepting investigative reports for fears of libel suits, while free-speech advocates like MediaRights.org no longer allow the sharing of films, but only databases and messages, to avoid copyright infringement.[37] These restrictions may grow as U.S. courts give freelancers retroactive electronic rights, further limiting the free use of material on the Web.[38] It is also worth remembering that "fair use" may be more easily claimed for "creative" work than for factual material in the wake of the U.S. Napster rulings,[39] leaving documentary in a sort of legal gray zone.

Corporate productions may be less varied in a digital age, whatever efforts are made toward "rationalized diversity." Convergence has resulted in job layoffs at many of the major networks and given rise to new forms of "multitasking" in which individual producers are expected to engage in a wide array of publishing, reporting, and filmmaking activities. This could work to the overall detriment of media diversity.[40] At the same time, digitalization may result in fewer original productions, particularly at the startup stage. The fact that only 20 percent of digital productions at BBC America are new, compared with 35 percent to 40 percent at the analog network, certainly suggests a less varied digital documentary lineup.[41] Similar patterns at DNI belie the oft-repeated claims that "digital allows you to take [documentary programming] into special interests."[42]

Online Texts: Article Z's *How Geraldo Lost His Job*

Clearly, then, a number of economic, legal, and technological hurdles impede the free flow of digital images across borders much as they did in the national broadcasting era. But that said, new factual technologies do seem to create significant spaces for public discussion and public action in the broadest sense of the term, and in this concluding section I want to examine how documentation might work in a postbroadcasting text— particularly in a text of a less corporate variety than the ones examined above.

How Geraldo Lost His Job is just such a text—a postbroadcasting, postnational project in every sense of those terms. Created by France's Article Z collective with the help of the ARTE channel, the *Geraldo* production is specifically designed for the Internet, as a Website dictated in part by the user. Here the online site serves as something more than a backup for a cut-and-dried broadcast product. At the same time, *Geraldo* is part of an avowedly global service—the One World Television Service network, which tackles ten world issues each year. Meanwhile, as a text, *Geraldo* approaches its subject in ways not seen on conventional television, with interactive story-telling designed to appeal to "younger audiences who have deserted global issue broadcasts in droves," according to founder Patrice Barrat.[43] *Geraldo* is a work in progress rather than a finished text, an investigation driven by ongoing interventions— by producers, subjects, and viewers. It is in these ways that One World sets out to investigate globalization at "the request of ordinary citizens."[44]

Geraldo begins with a question: Respondent Geraldo de Sousa wants to know why he lost his job at a Ford Motor plant in São Paulo, Brazil, in 1998. The program's Website opens with a brief scripted and spoken introduction outlining its subject's predicament and his desire to know "who made the decision and why." We are then introduced to American investigative reporter Jon Alpert, who will be "entirely at Geraldo's disposal" for the duration of the case, while responding to viewers along the way. A video clip presents Alpert showing Geraldo the mechanics of the networking technology and his conversations with various authorities on Brazilian employment. Ford refuses to appear, online or on-camera, so Alpert introduces a link entitled "other manufacturers, other mores" in which a Volkswagen executive outlines what he calls his company's "more social approach" to car production. If Geraldo had been working at the VW plant, we are told, he would still have a job, though perhaps one with reduced hours. Another segment entitled "where are the jobs" takes Alpert to the offices of Brazilian economist Robert da Costa, who advises Geraldo to look for work "outside of São Paulo, and perhaps outside of Brazil" as the country undergoes a difficult economic transition. Alpert then goes to Washington, D.C., to talk to representatives of the International Monetary Fund. Here a top official in the Latin American office tries to explain some "macroeconomic facts" in a "move to establish some sort of proximity with Geraldo." Brazil, the official argues, does not export enough and thus must raise interest rates in an effort to attract investors, which in turn discourages car buying, leading to layoffs such as Geraldo's. The situation is exacerbated by financial crises in Russia and Asia that make investors jittery and developing economies even more vulnerable. "So what happened on another side of the world had a direct impact on Geraldo's situation?" Alpert asks. "Very direct impact, no doubt about it," he is told.

The president of the Brazilian Workers Party (and now the president of Brazil) agrees that global forces are decisive, but he has different ideas about how to deal with them. In his view, global capital flows must be regulated to safeguard Brazilian jobs and protect the economy from waves of speculation and divestment. In this section, Geraldo himself asks the questions. The investigation concludes, at least tentatively, with a final clip of Geraldo back on the job at the Ford motor plant. After twelve months of investigation, claims the report, "Geraldo has not only understood the mechanisms leading to his layoff, he has a job again." What role One World played in all this—a fair question as just 3 percent of the Ford plant's workers were reinstated at the time Geraldo was—is left "up to viewers to decide."

In many ways, *Geraldo* is reminiscent of a conventional public affairs program, particularly in the way it investigates a local problem in search of wider meaning. Clearly, *Geraldo* represents places and public issues much like its predecessors in an earlier age but in many respects quite differently. First there is the determinedly global approach it takes to its local subject matter. *Geraldo* represents a locale—specifically a part of Brazil in the throes of economic crisis—but it does so in consistently "translocal" sorts of ways. "We use local stories," claims Article Z founder Patrice Barrat, "but for us it's a lever to get directly to the wider scope and tackle the [larger] institutions."[45] In the same way, One World generally uses local reporters to encourage open dialogue with its respondents, but it also features broader discussion forums to "allow people to connect with other communities around the world affected by the same issue."[46] Locality is the subject here, but it is conceived as a space of flows within an increasingly borderless world.

Article Z also allows public discussions but in mostly unconventional ways. Notably, productions adhere to a sort of unabashed infotainment style that is meant to be both "serious and entertaining" and consisting mostly of quest-based mysteries. People loom large as both personalities and public citizens. And spaces emerge as both evocative settings and institutional locales that allow plots to develop and arguments to proceed. Viewers are meant to enjoy *Geraldo* both ways—as enlightenment and detective story—and Article Z is perhaps more explicit and less apologetic about these possible modes of attachment than its public service forebears.

Geraldo and other Article Z productions make sense in a mostly nonlinear fashion. *Geraldo* is a largely participatory text that accumulates meaning and resonance through a series of interventions—on the part of viewers, producers, and of course respondents (insofar as these personages can be kept separate in the production process). Producers respond to the directions of subjects and viewers; the latter provide feedback; and all parties are encouraged to set up Websites of their own— making it increasingly unclear just who is the "author" and who the "recipient" of the program's meaning. At the same time, *Geraldo*'s facts are "true" but only provisionally so, enlarged upon through the actions of these various agents in the world at large in response to the core text itself. In short, *Geraldo* is anything but an open-and-shut case. Instead, it offers us a flexible text in progress that lets us know—and care about—our world in new, post-televisual ways.

Global Documentary Reconsidered

So what does this study of emerging structures and practices tell us about documentary today? That is, are these the best or worst of times for documentary programming? Does it even make sense to speak of a documentary "Golden Age"? Or is the "McDoc," with all its banality and all its sameness, a more appropriate global icon?

I hope we are now in a position to dismiss, or at least rethink, some of these questions in light of what we know about global documentary today. First, transnational flows of money, ideas, producers, and productions create a cultural environment that defies easy description and prescription. At the very least, documentaries now have a harder time representing clearly delineated places and public issues in a less bordered world; and as a result, they will only be properly understood with the help of new (and more nuanced) types of criticism. Neither public service nostalgia nor global market exuberance is of much help here.

Second, global documentary should be thought of as a transnational practice rather than a locally grounded set of texts. We should understand documentary as something more than a select group of films or programs emerging from particular countries or cultural traditions. Instead we should see documentary as what Larry Grossberg calls a "configuration of practices" with effects that can only be organized and activated in particular circumstances.[47] As such, documentary studies extend beyond bounded cultural analysis in a traditional sense. Rather than judging productions from some Archimedean vantage point—from which "authenticity" or "critical edge" is determined according to a fixed set of rules—we could consider the ways documentaries are deployed in emerging networks and consumed in new ways with varying repercussions. We could pay heed, that is, to both the situatedness and the mobility of documentary production. Global analysis, in this sense, would be a study of documentary in a fluid context, calling into question our traditional preoccupation with stable objects, standards, and meanings.

Of course this book hardly amounts to the full-fledged global analysis I am advocating. Much work remains to be done concerning the new productions, new distribution patterns, and new spaces of viewing that are still (and always) emerging in a transnational documentary marketplace. But that said, the thrust of a global analysis is clear: Engaging future documentaries will require rethinking our critical past and leaving behind the solid ground of documentary theory as we knew it in the national public service era. Taking leave in this sense is a first step in a global direction.

Notes

Chapter 1

1. "Documania on world market," *Television Business International*, 1999, June, 26. This view is current in industry circles as well. Former Time Warner CEO Gerald Levin contends that documentary is thriving on global specialty channels as it never did on network television. See "Upfront," 1999, *RealScreen*, July, 6. Meanwhile, the world's largest global television market, the Marché International des Programmes, has launched MIPDOC, a special documentary panel, to herald the "Golden Age" of documentary on global television. See Clarke, Steve. 1998. "Special report for MIPDOC," *RealScreen*, March, 24.

2. Maysles, Albert. 1998. "The defunct A roll," *RealScreen*, October, 96.

3. For more general discussions concerning "aesthetic reflexivity" on the part of cultural consumers see Lash, S. and Urry, J. 1994. *Economies of Signs and Spaces*. London: Sage.

4. Jacobs, Bert. 2000. "Reality schizoid," *Now Magazine*, June 29–July 5, 14.

5. See, for instance, McChesney, R.W. and Herman, E.S. 1997. *The Global Media*. London: Cassell.

6. For a critical survey of the European public service tradition see Winston, Brian. 1995. *Claiming the Real: Griersonian Documentary and Its Legitimations*. London: British Film Institute; and Corner, John. 1996. *The Art of Record*. Manchester, England: Manchester University Press. With respect to the North American public broadcasting tradition see Bullert, B.J. 2000. *Public Television: Politics in the Battle over Documentary*. New Brunswick, N.J.: Rutgers University Press; and Hogarth, David. 2002. *Documentary Television in Canada: From National Public Service to Global Marketplace*. Montreal: McGill-Queens University Press.

7. Interview with Sidney Newman, 17 October 1997. See also John Grierson's explication of the documentary public service tradition in the Commonwealth countries in Grierson, John. 1979. *Grierson on Documentary*. London: Faber and Faber.

8. See Bouse, Derek. 1998. "Are wildlife films really 'nature documentaries'?" *Critical Studies in Mass Communication* 15, no. 2 (June): 140.

9. See, for instance, Gaines, Jane M. 1999. "Introduction: The real returns," in Gaines, Jane M. and Renov, Michael (eds.), *Collecting Visible Evidence*, Minneapolis: University of Minnesota Press.

10. See "EDN attacks television," 2000, *DocTV*, 30 November. For similar trends in France see Television France International. 2001. *Synthèse des flux internationaux de la production française 2000*. Paris: TFI.

11. Dolman, Trish. 2000. "The future of the documentary one-off," *Independent*, March, 35–37.

12. Film has been eclipsed even at traditional venues, with just ten of more than two hundred documentary submissions at the 1999 Sundance Film Festival managing to obtain widespread theatrical release and more than three-fourths originating on broadcast-friendly videotape. See "Upfront," 1999, *RealScreen*, March, 6; and Binning, Cheryl. 1999. "Big screen docs: Pushing your own product," *RealScreen*, January, 87. Perhaps most tellingly in France—the heartland of the documentary film tradition—cinema screenings are now mostly limited to short runs in outlying areas, many of them sponsored by sympathetic broadcasters such as the ARTE channel. See Television France International (TFI). 2001. *Synthèse des flux internationaux de la production française 2000*. Paris: TFI.

The same trends are evident in production and distribution circles. Of sixteen documentaries competing at the 2002 Sundance Festival, eleven were produced for U.S. television networks, and the rest were scheduled to be released on the American HBO and PBS television networks. A *New York Times* writer has noted, "Even accomplished [American documentary] filmmakers are on their own if they cannot go to public television or HBO for money"; Pinkser, Beth. 2002. "Cash with strings for docs," *New York Times*, 14 January.

As for pockets of resistance, the influence of television can be seen as well. The Netherlands-based DocuZone project circulates films in innovative digital ways, but hardly any of these productions is made without the involvement of a broadcaster. See Ryninks, Kees. 2002. "DocuZone: A Dutch digital experiment," *Dox*, April, 9. Similarly, in Australia efforts to revive documentary cinema have been offset by what one observer calls the overall "reconfiguring" of the genre around television. See Roscoe, Jane. 2004. "Television and Australian documentary" *Media, Culture and Society* 26 (2): 288. And finally in the all-important American market, broadcasting continues to dominate, with notable cinema hits like Michael Moore's *Bowling for Columbine* earning DVD and television sales up to five times their box office receipts (many observers predict similar small-screen success for *Fahrenheit 911*, which may explain Moore's decision to take his film out of the Oscar race to hasten TV distribution). See Brown, Kimberley. 2004. "On to something," *RealScreen*, September, 9. Of course, the prestige of a theatrical documentary release remains undeniable. But increasingly, and in most ways, cinematic technologies are becoming marginal to the production and distribution of factual images.

13. Gabori, Susan. 1979. "MIP-TV: Programming the world," *Cinema Canada*, August, 29–31.

14. See, for instance, Felix Guattari's comments on factual television in Guattari, Felix. 1992. *Soft Subversions*. New York: Semiotext(e).

15. See, for instance, Gaines, Jane M. 1999. "Introduction: The real returns," in Gaines, Jane M. and Renov, Michael (eds.), *Collecting Visible Evidence*. Minneapolis: University of Minnesota Press; and some of the selections in Waldman, Diane and Walker, Janet (eds.), 1999. *Feminism and Documentary*. Minneapolis: University of Minnesota Press.

16. For the policy makers who presided over the introduction of television to Canada in 1952, public service broadcasting was chiefly distinguished by its documentary value, or as they put it, its "reproduction of real as opposed to synthetic situations." Canada. 1951. *Report of the Royal Commission on National Development in the Arts, Letters, and Sciences (Massey-Levesque)*. Ottawa: King's Printer, 51. For more formally minded critics, documentary programs offered a stylistic range unmatched by other genres, drawing upon drama, satire, and various modes of "progressive realism"; see, for instance, Gallant, Mavis. 1949. "Culture on the air," *Winnipeg Standard*, 8 October, 8. In both views, documentary television faithfully represented viewers while empowering them as citizens. More than any other genre, documentary was seen to engage a broad range of civic and cultural competencies.

Of course, the shows have also had their critics. For neoconservatives, the urge to document the nation with all its warts is proof that public broadcasting has run its course and lost its way in a cultural free market. And for deregulators the documentary impulse—the urge to make depressingly real shows that nobody wants to watch—helps explain public broadcasting's precarious position in an open, competitive playing field. In short, documentary has been at the center of various efforts to dismantle state-supported culture, particularly in Europe and the United States; see Winston, Brian. 2000. *Lies, Damn Lies and Documentary*. London: British Film Institute; and Bullert, B.J. 2000. *Public Television: Politics in the Battle over Documentary*. New Brunswick, N.J.: Rutgers University Press; and Hogarth, David. 2002. *Documentary Television in Canada*. Montreal: McGill-Queens University Press. But castigated or celebrated, documentary is still widely regarded as a defining genre of public broadcasting.

17. See, for instance, Kilborn, Richard. 1996. "New contexts in documentary production in Britain," *Media, Culture and Society* 18 (2): 141–150.

18. Singapore Broadcast Authority Public Advisory Committee cited in Kunothangan, Gladius D. 2000. "Media content in Asia: More waste or substance?" *Media Asia* 26 (3): 17.

19. Doyle, John. 2001. "CBC takes itself seriously but in a serious way," *Globe and Mail*, 11 June, R.

20. The critical reception of the Canadian Broadcasting Corporation's millennial documentary project, "Canada: A People's History" (CPH), is a case in point. On its 2000 release, the program was widely celebrated as a "seminal project" that would demonstrate the worth of public broadcasting. For columnist John MacLachlan Gray the program "exemplified a near extinct form called public television." See Gray, John MacLachlan. 2000. "Canada: A People's alienation," *Globe and Mail*, 27 December, R. And for critic John Doyle the program "saved CBC television from a fate worse than death—irrelevancy." See Doyle, John. 2001. "A People's History from a hoser's perspective," *Globe and Mail*, 4 January, R.

But CPH was also seen as a cultural test in a broader sense, as an opportunity for Canada to prove its cultural distinctiveness in a world without borders. "It turns out 2 1/2 million wanted a history lesson," crowed one critic in response to predictions that Canadians no longer cared about national stories. See Gray, John MacLachlan. 2000. "Canada: A People's alienation," *Globe and Mail*, 27 December, R. In the view of many critics, the nation had an ongoing duty to document itself because it was different while at the same time demonstrating its difference by documenting itself—with Canada's difference lying in its refusal to indulge in American televisual escapism. Documentary has thus always assumed a heavy rhetorical burden in national public service discourse. That is, it has done double duty as both a record and a ritual of national identity.

21. Curran, James. 1999. "The crisis of public communication: A

reappraisal," in Liebes, Tamar and Curran, James (eds.) *Media, Ritual and Identity.* London: Routledge.

22. *Ibid.*, 189.

23. Sparks, Colin. 1998. "Is there a global public sphere?" in Thussu, Daya, ed., *Electronic Empires: Global Media and Local Resistance.* London: Edward Arnold.

24. See, for instance, Hoskins, Colin and McFadyen, Stuart. 1993. "Canadian participation in international coproductions and co-ventures in television programming," *Canadian Journal of Communication* 18 (fall): 219–236.

25. Havens, Timothy. 2000. "The biggest show in the world: Race and the global popularity of the Cosby show," *Media, Culture and Society* 22 (4): 371–391.

26. See, for instance, Kilborn, Richard. 1996. "New contexts in documentary production in Britain," *Media, Culture and Society* 18 (2): 141–150.

27. See chapter 2 of this volume along with the statistics compiled in Vista Advisers for RAI. 2001. *The Documentary Market Worldwide.* Rome: RAI. The latter study does forecast brisk growth rates for the genre around the world, however.

28. As Brian Winston has noted in Winston, Brian. 2000. *Lies, Damn Lies and Documentary,* London: British Film Institute. Specialty channels may not remain bit players for long, however. As the authors of one recent market survey argue, "popular documentaries" may be "potentially vulnerable to competitive encroachment by niche thematic channels in the digital age." David Graham and Associates. 2000. *Out of the Box: A Report for the Department of Culture, Media and Sport.* Taunton, England: U.K. Department of Culture, Media, and Sport, 42. At the same time, documentaries seem to be making inroads on the specialty channels themselves. One report suggests that documentary channels were actually the fastest-growing service on UK cable and satellite services, with audience share growing from 0.4 percent in 1991 to 2.1 percent in 1999. "Kids oust movies as TV demographics evolve," 1999, *Screen Digest,* July, 14.

29. David Graham and Associates. 2000. *British Television: The Global Market Challenge.* London: British Television Directors Association. See also Vista Advisers for RAI. 2001. *The Documentary Market Worldwide.* Rome: RAI, 38.

30. Vista Advisers for RAI. 2001. *The Documentary Market Worldwide.* Rome: RAI, 37.

31. New on the Air (NOTA). 2001. *Yearly Report.* www.e-nota .com/reports.

32. Appadurai, Arjun. 1996. *Modernity at Large.* Minneapolis: University of Minnesota Press, 3.

33. Swedish producer Bo Landin cited in Kennedy, John. 1998. "Producer profiles: Scandinature Films," *RealScreen*, August, 16.

34. Bauman, Zygmunt. 1995. *Life in Fragments.* Oxford, England: Blackwell, 24.

35. Dovey, Jon. 2000. *Freakshow: First Person Media and Factual Television.* London: Pluto Press, 151.

36. Steven, Peter. 1992. *Brink of Reality: New Canadian Documentary Film and Video.* Toronto: Between the Lines.

37. Zimmermann, Patricia R. 2000. *States of Emergency: Documentaries, Wars, Democracies.* Minneapolis: University of Minnesota Press, 11.

38. Roscoe, Jane. 2001. "Australian documentary: Safe in the hands of the next generation," *Dox*, August, 11.

39. Bruzzi, Stella. 2000. *New Documentary: A Critical Introduction.* London: Routledge. Similarly, Gaines and Renov's "significant reconfiguration" of documentary studies (p. 1) devotes only one chapter specifically to television. See Williams, Mark. 1999. "History in a flash: Notes on the myth of TV liveness," in Gaines, Jane M. and Renov, Michael (eds.), *Collecting Visible Evidence.* Minneapolis: University of Minnesota Press: 292–312. Even this is hardly an "update," as it consists mostly of Korean War case studies.

40. Zimmermann, Patricia R. 2000. *States of Emergency: Documentaries, Wars, Democracies.* Minneapolis: University of Minnesota Press. Zimmermann deliberately omits transnational documentary channels such as Discovery and A&E on the grounds that "they secure ample space in TV guide and sufficient airtime" (p. xx). All the more reason to critique them, one might argue, as global cultural forces arguably shape American public space just as decisively as the domestic political actors whom Zimmermann targets.

41. Longfellow, Brenda. 1996. "Globalization and national identity in Canadian film," *Canadian Journal of Film Studies* 5, no. 2 (fall): 3–16. Feldman observes that Canadian documentaries are "assiduously searched for signs of national identity" by film critics; Feldman, Seth. 1983. "The electronic fable: Aspects of the docudrama in Canada," *Canadian Drama* 8 (2): 41.

42. Here I exclude some notable studies of international documentary film and television. See, for instance, Brigitte Hahn's study of U.S. documentary propaganda and its effect on German political culture; Hahn, Brigitte J. 1997. *Umerziehung durch Dokumentarfilm? ein Instrument amerikanischer Kulturpolitik im nach-Kriegsdeutschland (1945–1953).* Munster, Germany: Lit; and Izod et al.'s study of the in-

fluence of Grierson on documentary film and television around the world in Izod, John, Kilborn, Richard and Hibberd, Matthew. 2000. *From Grierson to the Docu-Soap: Breaking the Boundaries.* Luton, England: University of Luton Press, 2000. But even these studies focus on nation-states, or the orderly exchange of documentary films between them. They are hardly concerned with "global" documentaries as I have defined them.

43. Verna, Tony. 1996. *Global Television: How to Create Effective Television for the Future.* London: Longman.

44. Barker, Chris. 1997. *Global Television: An Introduction.* Oxford, England: Blackwell. Documentary may have been dismissed as an exception to televisual "rules." After all, the genre is neither live nor ephemeral nor popular in rating terms. Furthermore, it often focuses on abstract social issues rather than the down-to-earth domestic matters that are seen to be the stuff of broadcasting. In other words, documentary lacks many of the characteristics associated with televisuality.

45. See Winston, Brian. 1995. *Claiming the Real: The Griersonian Documentary and its Legitimations.* London: British Film Institute; Corner, John. 1996. *The Art of Record,* Manchester, England: Manchester University Press; and Kilborn, Richard, and Izod, John. 1999. *An Introduction to Television Documentary.* Manchester, England: Manchester University Press. Winston does offer an insightful analysis of international copyright regimes, however. See Winston, Brian. 2000. *Lies, Damn Lies and Documentary.* London: British Film Institute.

The public service perspective can result in a narrow and rather unforgiving view of global market products. Kilborn, for instance, has dismissed docusoaps as an American "dumbing down" of the traditional Griersonian documentary (though he seems to have modified his stance of late). See Kilborn, Richard. 1994. "How real can you get? Recent developments in reality television," *European Journal of Communication* 9 (3): 421–439.

46. Dauncey, Hugh. 1996. "French reality television: More than a matter of taste," *European Journal of Communication* 11 (1): 94; and Glynn, K. 2000. *Tabloid Culture: Trash Taste, Popular Power, and the Transformation of American Television.* Durham, N.C.: Duke University Press, 2. Fishman also notes "considerable intra-genre diversity" in American reality-based crime shows. See Fishman, Jessica M. 1999. "The populace and the police in reality-based crime TV," *Critical Studies in Mass Communication* (16): 268–288; quote is on p. 282.

47. Producers tend to distinguish between documentary and reality shows according to circumstances. In the United States, for in-

stance, producers of cop shows and tabloid news programs sometimes call them documentaries to claim "fair use" of archival footage—an exemption not available to entertainment producers. See Christie, Brendan. 1998. "The difference between rights and wrongs," *Real-Screen*, March, 37; and Blumenthal, Howard J. and Goodenough, Oliver. 1998. *The Business of Television.* 2d ed. New York: Billboard Books, 195–196. American producers also seek documentary certification because the 1996 U.S. Telecommunications Act excludes some forms of news and documentary programming from its V-chip ratings system; see Whitney, D. Charles, Wartella, Ellen, Lasorsa, Domenic and Danielson, Wayne. 1999. "Monitoring 'reality' television: The national television violence study," in Nordenstrong, Kaarle and Griffin, Michael (eds.) *International Media Monitoring.* Cresskill, N.J.: Hampton Press, 371. Meanwhile, Canadian and British producers seek to have current affairs productions counted as documentaries to fulfill public service quotas; see Canadian Television Fund (CTF). 1999. *Documentary Programming Module 1999.* Ottawa: CTF, 2; and Winston, Brian. 2000. *Lies, Damn Lies and Documentaries.* London: British Film Institute. 102–104. Similarly, their American counterparts at the HBO network sometimes call their extended investigative reports "news" to avoid gaining release forms from subjects; see Keenlyside, Sarah. 2000. "Please release me," *RealScreen*, October, 56.

For their part, policy makers tend to take a more fixed view. Canadian tax acts, for instance, specifically exclude reality productions from their credit systems. See Houle, Michel. 2000. *Documentary Production in Quebec and Canada, 1991/2–1998/9: Phase 1,* www.ridm.qc.ca. Similarly, the Australian Film Finance Corporation will not invest in reality or infotainment programs, which it differentiates from documentaries. See Australian Film Finance Corporation (AFFC). 2002. *Investment Guidelines 2001/2.* Sydney: AFFC. In all these cases, however, classifications serve a functional purpose that allows for some flexibility. That is, they are subject to change over time.

48. Ellis, John. 2000. "Scheduling: The last creative act in television," *Media, Culture and Society* 22 (2): 25–38. As Ellis sees it, schedules have not simply put the programs in order; they have ordered the programs (p. 33).

49. Producer Olivier Bremond cited in Hood, Duncan. 1998. "Marathon's race to the top," *RealScreen*, September, 23. Though some foreign competitors avoid the documentary label altogether, American producers often note the network's aversion to "the D-word"; one long-time supplier even describes his work as "entertaining programs for kids which have a commitment to real world content." Producer Colin

Nobbs cited in Brown, Kimberley. 2001. "S is for science," *RealScreen*, October, 95. European producers, on the other hand, may shun the term to avoid the long arm of the European Broadcasting Union, which apparently wants to define children's documentaries so it can regulate them. See Kjeldsen, Klaus. 2001. "Docs in a kid's perspective," *Dox*, December, 21.

50. See Woodward, Leslie. 2000. "Documentary as a casualty of the ratings war," *DocTV*, 4 September, 2.

Chapter 2

1. For a review of these problems see Auguson, Preta, De Angelis, Maria and Mazzotti, Maria. 1996. *The Quest for Quality: Survey on Television Viewing Scheduling Worldwide*. Rome: RAI, General Secretariat of Prix Italia, 43, 56.

2. The United Kingdom promises to collect some of this information in the near future, and France already does. See David Graham and Associates. 2000. *Building a Global Audience: British Television in Overseas Markets*. Taunton, England: U.K. Department of Culture, Media, and Sport. See also Television France International (TFI). 2001. *Synthèse des flux internationaux de la production française 2000*. Paris: TFI.

3. As a number of market studies have acknowledged; see, for instance, David Graham and Associates. 2000. *Out of the Box: Report for the Department of Culture, Media and Sport*. Taunton, England: U.K. Department of Culture, Media, and Sport

4. As Canadian statisticians note, many producers engage in co-ventures rather than official coproductions precisely to avoid such paperwork. This is especially the case with independent producers, who tend to be Canada's most aggressive exporters, meaning that global production is routinely underrepresented in Canadian reports. Interview with Mark Davis, Price Waterhouse Cooper, 30 September 2001.

5. Bauman, Zygmunt. 1995. *Life in Fragments*. Oxford, England: Blackwell, 24.

6. Tomlinson, John. 1999. *Globalization and Culture*. Chicago: University of Chicago Press.

7. See Sparks, Colin. 1998. "Is there a global public sphere?" in Daya Thussu, ed., *Electronic Empires: Global Media and Local Resistance*. London: Edward Arnold, 108–124.

8. New on the Air (NOTA). 2001. *Yearly Report*. wwww.e-nota .com/reports.

9. See, for instance, Richardson, Kay and Meinhof, Ulrike A. 1999. *Worlds in Common: Television Discourse in a Changing Europe*. London: Routledge.

10. Kilborn, Richard. 1996. "New contexts for documentary production in Britain," *Media, Culture and Society* 18 (2): 142.

11. Winston, Brian. 2000. *Lies, Damn Lies and Documentary*. London: British Film Institute.

12. Catherine Lim, assistant vice-president of local commissioning, STV 12, cited in Hazan, Jenny. 2001. "Singapore Television 12," *RealScreen*, January, 36.

13. "Finnish television seeks world programming," 2001, *Docos .com*, 26 January.

14. Cleasby, Adrian. 1995. *What in the world is going on?: British television and Global Affairs*. London: Third World and Environmental Broadcasting Project, iii.

15. See the Website www.ePolitix.com/EN/forums. In chapters 4 and 5 I question what these studies mean by a "hard look."

16. TV New Zealand's Natural History Unit was purchased by Rupert Murdoch's News Corporation in 1999.

17. Kuzmyk, Jenn. 1999. "Hot Docs welcomes the world," *Playback*, 23 May, 23.

18. Interview with Chris Haws, Discovery Channel, 18 October 2001.

19. Richardson, Kay and Meinhof, Ulrike A. 1999. *Worlds in Common: Television Discourse in a Changing Europe*. London: Routledge, 106.

20. Ellis, John. 2000. "Scheduling: the last creative act in television?" *Media, Culture and Society* 22 (2): 36.

21. Interview with Philip Hampson, 20 July 2001.

22. Interview with Chris Haws, Discovery Channel, 18 October 2001.

23. Hogarth, David. 2001. "Communication Policy in a Global Age," in Burke, Mike, Mooers, Colin and Shields, John (eds.) *Restructuring and Resistance*. Toronto: Fernwood Press.

24. See *IDA Source Book* for examples.

25. Interview with Chris Haws, Discovery Channel, 18 October 2001.

26. FOCAL International helps clear foreign rights and provides legal advice regarding documentary footage. See Rayman, Susan. 2001. "Culling the Shots," *RealScreen*, February, 39.

27. See, for instance, Conlogue, Ray. 2001. "Culture is a blood sport," *Globe and Mail*, May 1, A. In fact, twelve of fifteen European

Union countries have given in to U.S. pressure and opened their markets to documentaries and other cultural products.

28. Vista Advisers for RAI. 2001. *The Documentary Market Worldwide*. Rome: RAI, 37.

29. *Ibid.*, 39.

30. Kuzmyk, Jenn. 1998. "MIP-Asia: Fighting the Flu," *RealScreen*, December, 44. Wildlife imagery is particularly marketable in this regard.

31. See Dubois, Julien. 1999. "Documentaries in France," *RealScreen*, June, 3. More than 90 percent of France's documentaries were funded domestically in 1998, and coproductions and pre-sales accounted for less than 7 percent of home productions. See Centre National de la Cinématographie. 2000. *Statistiques Annuelles 2000: Cinéma, Audio-Visuel, Television, Video, Multimedia*, 17 May.

32. Vista Advisers for RAI. 2001. *The Documentary Market Worldwide*. Rome: RAI, 37.

33. *Ibid.*

34. Simpson, Jeffrey. 2002. "Watching the bigger picture through US eyes," *Globe and Mail*, 6 February, A.

35. "Australian documentary production figures released," 2000, *Docos.com*, 14 November.

36. Australian Film Commission/Film Finance Corporation. 1999. *Report on the Film and Television Production Industry*. Sydney: Minister of the Arts and Centenary Federation, 48.

37. Australian Broadcast Authority (ABA). 2000. *Investigation into Expenditure Requirements for PAY-TV Documentary Channels*. Sydney: ABA, 19. The report finds that prices for domestic free-to-air documentaries ranged between Aus$21,465 and Aus$25,000, compared with the Aus$2,164 and Aus$7,000 per hour paid for imported programs by pay-TV channels. It concluded that the "availability of large amounts of cheaper foreign product" was the chief means by which specialty channels competed for the domestic market. Australian Film Commission/Film Finance Corporation. 1999. *Report on the Film and Television Production Industry*. Sydney: Minister of the Arts and Centenary Federation, 48.

38. Mazurkewich, Karen. 1999. "Aussie and Kiwi prodcos look outward," *RealScreen*, December, 35.

39. Hazan, Jenny. 2001. "The Israeli Filmmaking Front," *RealScreen*, June, 36.

40. Cowern, Christine. 1999. "Channel 8," *RealScreen*, July, 18.

41. Mazurkewich, Karen. 1999. "The view from here: Spotlight on Hong Kong," *RealScreen*, November, 30.

42. Powers, Thom. 2000. "China's undiscovered wildlife," *Real-Screen*, August, 68.

43. *Ibid.*

44. Hughes, Nancy. 1999. "Latin lovers," *RealScreen*, May, 50–53.

45. Cited in Raphael, Jordan. 2001. "Bona fide Brazil," *RealScreen*, October, 44.

46. Vista Advisers for RAI. 2001. *The Documentary Market Worldwide.* Rome: RAI, 54.

47. "Intertel 1963," *CBC Times*, 5–11 January: 4.

48. *Ibid.*

49. For a brief history of the international exchange of documentary films see the preamble to Statistics Canada. 1998. *Tabulations of Documentaries 1995-7.* Ottawa: Minister of Supply and Services, 1.

50. See also Hogarth, David. 2002. *Documentary Television in Canada: From National Public Service to Global Marketplace.* Montreal: McGill-Queens University Press.

51. *Ibid.*

52. Koch, Eric. 1991. *Inside Seven Days.* Scarborough, Ontario: Prentice-Hall, 20.

53. Canadian Broadcasting Corporation (CBC). 1972. "Area Heads Meeting," CBC internal memo. 16 February. CBC National Archives Papers, RG 41, Series A-V-2, Volume 894/File T1-3-2-7/Pt. 6, TV Information Programming—Current Affairs, 1970–72.

54. Nixon, Doug. 1961. *Minutes: CBC National Conference Outside Broadcasts Department.* 27 November–1 December: 15. CBC National Archives Papers, RG 41, Series A-V-2, Volume 851, PG1–13, Pt. 3.

55. Production dropped off, however, after a Cold War flurry of activity, which suggests the programs served political as well as commercial ends. See Curtin, Michael. 1993. *Redeeming the Wasteland: Television Documentary and Cold War Politics.* New Brunswick, N.J.: Rutgers University Press.

56. Freeson, Andrew. 1998. "Social issue docs hard sell in Cannes," *New York Times*, 13 April, F.

57. McGreery, John. 1998. "Peter Ustinov's Russia," *Toronto Star*, 2 March, D.

58. Allemang, John. 1998. "Passing judgement on TV's best at Banff festival," *Globe and Mail*, 16 June, C.

59. Vista Advisers for RAI. 2001. *The Documentary Market Worldwide.* Rome: RAI, 21.

60. Christie, Brendan. 2001. "By the numbers," *RealScreen*, March, 38.

61. *Ibid.*

62. "In my opinion," 2001, *RealScreen*, June, 38.

63. Jordan, Raphael. 2001. "Bona Fide Brazil," *RealScreen*, October, 44.

64. Sanda Rich cited in Brown, Kimberley. 2001. "New IDA head wants to raise profile of docs," *RealScreen*, July, 12.

65. Hazan, Jenny. 2001. "The EBU," *RealScreen*, March, 44.

66. Jan Rofekamp cited in Goodman, Robert M. 2000. "Is Content King?" *Independent*, November, 38–39.

67. This is compared with the 23 percent/36 percent market share of their national terrestrial counterparts. See Vista Advisers for RAI. 2001. *The Documentary Market Worldwide.* Rome: RAI, 39.

68. Rofekamp, Jan. 2000. "The future of the auteur doc," *Dox*, December, 1.

69. Zeller, Susan. 2001. "Reflecting on features," *RealScreen*, September, 6.

70. Interview with Michaela McLean, Hot Docs Documentary Forum director, 21 September 2001.

71. MacDonald, Gayle. 2001. "Hot Docs festival a global affair," *Globe and Mail*, 11 April, R.

72. Rayman, Susan and Christie, Brendan. 2000. "MIP mania," *RealScreen*, May, 12.

73. Kirchdoerffer, Ed. 1999. "NATPE: Not just for Oprah anymore," *RealScreen*, January, 64.

74. Interview with Michael Wang, independent Hong Kong filmmaker, 4 October 2000.

75. Hazan, Jenny. 2001. "Getting global," *RealScreen*, March, 69.

76. "European storytellers," 2002, *Dox*, June, 6.

77. MacDonald, Gayle. 2001. "Hot Docs festival a global affair," *Globe and Mail*, 11 April, R.

78. See www.d-film.com.

79. Hot Docs claims that more than 50 percent of its project pitches receive global funding. Interview with Michaela McLean, director of Hot Docs Documentary Forum, 21 September 2001.

80. Hazan, Jenny. 2001. "Getting global," *RealScreen*, March, 69.

81. Sanda Rich cited in Brown, Kimberley. 2001. "New IDA head wants to raise profile of docs," *RealScreen*, July, 12.

82. "INPUT prepares conference for South Africa," 2001, *Dox*, March, 4.

83. "Antics in the attic," 2001, *Economist*, 26 May, 63. Television rights are hard to defend internationally, as titles and project plans must be registered in each country.

84. Fishman, Mark and Calendar, Gary. 1998. "Television reality

crime programs," in Fishman, Mark and Calendar, Gary (eds.) *Entertaining Crime: Television Reality Programs.* New York: Aldine de Gruyter, 4.

85. Schlesinger, Philip and Tumbler, Howard. 1994. *Reporting Crime: The Media Politics of Criminal Justice.* Oxford, England: Clarendon Press, 251–252.

86. New on the Air (NOTA). 2001. *Yearly Report.* www.e-nota .com/reports.

87. McCann, P. 2001. "Everyone's watching Big Brother," *(London) Times,* 3 May, 3. Some market observers predicted the reality wave had crested by 2001, while others insisted the genre had become a fixed TV staple. At the very least the reality format seems to have changed fact and fiction programming in a lasting way.

88. Dovey, Jon. 2000. *Freakshow: First Person Media and Factual Television.* London: Pluto Press.

89. While an Amsterdam court eventually ruled that the Castaway and Endemol formats were demonstrably different, the case may continue as Castaway lays similar charges against the BBC and Channel 4. See "Court backs Big Brother, maroons Castaway," 2001, *Docos .com,* 9 June. Even if the formats are demonstrably different, those differences may not hold up in court. Some critics insist judges are unable to spot differences because they "don't watch enough TV" and "wouldn't know a cartoon from a documentary," as one producer puts it. David Lyle, Pearson Television (United Kingdom), cited in Rayman, Susan. 2001. "The second coming of formats," *RealScreen,* January, 55.

90. *Ibid.*

91. Peter van de Bussche cited in *ibid.*

92. Carter, Bill. 2001. "Reality TV: Have we created a monster?" *Globe and Mail,* 18 July, R.

93. *Ibid.*

94. Rayman, Susan. 2001. "The second coming of formats," *RealScreen,* January, 55.

95. Sassen, Saskia. 2001. in Appadurai, Arjun (ed.) *Globalization.* Durham, N.C.: Duke University Press.

Chapter 3

1. Australian Film Finance Corporation and Australian Film Commission. 2000. *Submission to the Australian Broadcasting Authority, Investigation into Expenditure Requirements for the PAY-TV Documentary Channels.* Sydney: ABA.

2. Public Broadcasting Service. 2001. Pacific Islanders in Communications guidelines. http://piccom.org.

3. Canadian Television Fund (CTF). 2001. *Documentary Programming Module, 2000-2001.* Ottawa: CTF, 1.

4. "Input prepares conference for South Africa," 2001, *Docos .com*, 3 May.

5. Anonymous official of New Zealand on the Air cited in Kirchdoerffer, Ed. 1999. "New Zealand's Hot Doc Makers," *RealScreen*, December, 40.

6. Clarke, Steve. 2001. "Finding Eire time for documentaries," *RealScreen*, September, 32.

7. Australian Broadcasting Authority (ABA). 2000. *Investigation into Expenditure Requirements for the PAY-TV Documentary Channels.* Sydney: ABA, 35.

8. Australian Film Finance Corporation (AFFC). 2001. *Investment Guidelines 2001/2.* Sydney: AFFC, 14.

9. The Canadian Radio-television and Telecommunications Commission suggests "Canadian" documentaries can consist of "images of Hiroshima and the moon" because these have become a "part of the Canadian heritage." The boundaries of documentary places and cultures have always been hard to define with any bureaucratic precision. See Canadian Radio-television and Telecommunications Commission. 2000. *Public Notice, 2000-42*, 1.

10. "Upfront: Nonfiction news," 1999, *RealScreen*, September, 6.

11. Cohen, Barri. 2000. *The Canadian Perspective: In Search of a Definition.* Toronto: Canadian Independent Film Caucus, 4.

12. "Aus deal signals theatrical doc screenings," 2000, *DocTV*, 24 August.

13. Public Broadcasting Service. 2001. Pacific Islanders in Communications guidelines. http://piccom.org.

14. Martyn Burke cited in Saunders, Doug. 1997. "Exporting Canadian culture," *Globe and Mail*, 25 January, C.

15. *Ibid.*

16. Susan McKinnon cited in Hazan, Jenny. 2001. "Getting global," *RealScreen*, March, 69.

17. John Kastner cited in Saunders, Doug. 1997. "Exporting Canadian culture," *Globe and Mail*, 25 January, C.

18. Sharon Connolly cited in Hazan, Jenny. 2001. "Getting global," *RealScreen*, March, 69.

19. Bouse, Derek. 1998. "Are wildlife films really 'nature documentaries'?" *Critical Studies in Mass Communication* 15, no. 2 (June): 133.

20. Jean-Noelle Robyn cited in "Natural History Guide: Odyssey," 1998, *RealScreen*, August, 18.

21. Michael Kott cited in Saunders, Doug. 1997. "Exporting Canadian culture," *Globe and Mail*, 25 January, C.

22. *Ibid.*

23. Interview with Philip Hampson, 20 July 2001.

24. Pawel Pawlikowski cited in MacDonald, Kevin and Cousins, Mark (eds.), 1996. *Imagining Reality: The Faber Book of the Documentary*. London: Faber and Faber, 388.

25. Chris Terrill cited in Paget, Derek. 1998. *No Other Way to Tell It*. Manchester, England: Manchester University Press, 94.

26. Richard Key cited in Fry, Andy. 1999. "Around the World in 3650 Days," *RealScreen*, February, 74.

27. Interview with Philip Hampson, 20 July 2001.

28. Rayman, Susan. 2001. "The Second Coming of Formats," *RealScreen*, January, 55.

29. Dovey, Jon. 2000. *Freakshow: First Person Media and Factual Television*. London: Pluto Press, 102.

30. Paget, Derek. 1998. *No Other Way to Tell It*. Manchester, England: Manchester University Press, 58.

31. Jacques Bidou cited in Baus, Emma. 2001. "Enabling coproductions," *Dox*, December, 8.

32. Interview with Kirwan Cox, 21 September 2001. Regarding the possibility for U.N. protection of local documentation projects see Smiers, Joost. 2004. "A convention on cultural diversity: From WTO to UNESCO," *Media International Australia* 111 (May): 81–96.

33. Allison, Peter. 1997. "Export market for doc programs heats up," *Playback*, 19 March, 20.

34. Dovey, Jon. 2000. *Freakshow: First Person Media and Factual Television*. London: Pluto Press, 133.

35. March, Catherine Dawson. 2001. "Harsh reality show," *Globe Television*, 9–15 June, 4–5.

36. Interview with Chris Haws, Discovery Channel, 18 October 2001.

37. Chris Haws cited in Fry, Andy. 1999. "Around the world in 3650 days," *RealScreen*, February, 74.

38. Interview with Chris Haws, Discovery Channel, 18 October 2001.

39. *Ibid.*

40. John Hendricks cited in Kirchdoerffer, Ed. 1997. "Tribute: Exploring John Hendricks' world," *RealScreen*, September, 53.

41. Joyce Taylor cited in Fry, Andy. 1999. "Around the world in 3650 days," *RealScreen*, February, 74.

42. *Ibid.*

43. Anonymous official cited in "Discovery US takes 33% of content from UK," 2000, *Docos.com*, 22 September.

44. Rick Rodriguez cited in Christie, Brendan. 1998. "The lowdown on localism: Fees and what sells," *RealScreen*, May, 30.

45. Kirchdoerffer, Ed. 1997. "Tribute: Exploring John Hendrick's world," *RealScreen*, September, 53.

46. Marjorie Kaplan cited in "News in brief," 2001, *RealScreen*, 17 October, 2.

47. Australian Broadcasting Authority. 2000. *Investigation into Expenditure Requirements for PAY-TV Documentary Channels*, 35.

48. Patrick Hoerll cited in Brown, Kimberley. 2000. "Discovery Producers' Workshop results in contracts," *RealScreen*, March, 6.

49. *Ibid.*

50. Discovery Campus Masterschool 2002, www.discovery-campus.de. The network also advises its interns that "a project does not get 'international' by simply setting it in various territories."

51. Fry, Andy. 1998. "Buyer profiles: Animal Planet Europe," *RealScreen*, August, 41.

52. Don Wear cited in Fry, Andy. 1999. "Around the world in 3650 days," *RealScreen*, February, 74.

53. Kevin-John McIntyre cited in *ibid.*

54. Armstrong, Mary Ellen. 1998. "Buyer profiles: National Geographic International," *RealScreen*, August, 44.

55. John Panickar, commissioning editor, Discovery Channel, Hot Docs 1998 industry conference, 20 March 1998.

56. Interview with Chris Haws, Discovery Channel, 18 October 2001.

57. *Ibid.*

58. During, Simon. 1997. "Popular culture on a global scale: A challenge for cultural studies?" *Critical Inquiry* 23 (summer): 809. See also Robertson, Roland. 1994. "Globalization or Glocalization?" *Journal of International Communication* 1, no. 1 (June): 33–53.

59. Andreef, M. 1999. "Adventure film outfit takes on TV," *Globe and Mail*, 15 March, B.

60. Reveler, Norma. 1998. "Turning a Documentary into a world marketing venture," *Marketing Magazine*, 20–27 July, 8.

61. *Hot Docs '98 Handbook.* 1998. Hot Docs festival, 45, 70.

62. Berland, Jody. 1993. "Sounds, image and social space: Music video and media reconstruction," in Frith, Simon, Goodwin, Andrew and Grossberg, Lawrence (eds.). *Sound and Vision: The Music Video Reader.* London and New York: Routledge, 37. Consider also the instrumental importance of place in nature documentaries, which seem

to be regarded by sponsors as vehicles to promote tourist industries and high-definition television (HDTV) sets rather than local documents per se. Promotional purposes aside, it seems unlikely that the genre is a hot seller because of any incipient demand for local documentation. Many observers point to a hunger for visual stimulation on the part of audiences and cheap programming on the part of broadcasters. See, for instance, Mrozek, Carl. 1998. "Technology: Nature in high definition," *RealScreen*, August, 26–32.

63. *Africa* was later shown on Discovery digital services in overseas markets.

64. Leakey developed the concept at length in his book *Wildlife Wars*, which was also the touchstone for a number of programs about Africa on the American PBS network and on the British Channel 4 service in 2001; Leakey, Richard and Morell, Virginia. 2001. *Wildlife Wars: My Fight to Save Africa's Natural Treasures*. New York: St. Martin's Press.

65. Interview with Doug Crosbie, 13 September 2001.

66. Interview with Jane Mingay, 18 September 2001.

67. Interview with Doug Crosbie, 13 September 2001.

68. For a contrary view of corporate culture and local diversity in the music business see Negus, Keith. 1999. *Music Genres and Corporate Culture*. London: Routledge, 154–155. In *Global Hollywood*, Miller et al. similarly argue that Hollywood dominates film to the detriment of local film cultures; Miller, Toby, Govil, Nitin, McMurria, John and Maxwell, Richard. 2001. *Global Hollywood*. London: British Film Institute.

Chapter 4

1. See Thompson, John B. 1997. "Tradition and self in a mediated world," in Heelas, Paul, Lash, Scott and Morriset, Paul (eds.), *Detraditionalization: Critical Reflections on Authority and Identity*. Oxford, England: Blackwell; and McGuigan, Jim. 1996. *Culture and the Public Sphere*. London: Routledge.

2. See, for instance, McLaughlin, Lisa. 1993. "Feminism, the public sphere, media and democracy," *Media, Culture and Society* 15 (3): 599–620.

3. See Winston, Brian. 2000. *Lies, Damn Lies and Documentary*. London: British Film Institute.

4. See Maysles, Albert. 1998. "The defunct A roll," *RealScreen*, October, 96.

5. Alex Graham cited in Rayman, Susan. 1999. "The health front," *RealScreen*, October, 44.

6. Rayman, Susan. 1999. "A view to a sale: The Middle East," *RealScreen*, March, 14.

7. Pottinger, Mark. 2000. "China bans Turner Broadcasting's network from its TV," *National Post* (Canada), 4 February, C11.

8. Interview with Chris Haws, Discovery Channel, 18 October 2001.

9. See Winston, Brian. 2000. *Lies, Damn Lies and Documentary.* London: British Film Institute.

10. See, for instance, the Independent Television Commission (ITC). 2001. *Programme Code.* London: ITC, 21–22.

11. See BBC's pledge at www.bbc.co.uk/info, especially chapter 7. A recent survey of global media regulations concludes that "at present there is no regulation to ensure that alongside private transnational media there could be transnational media for the public interest." However, the authors do contend that U.N. media resolutions have some moral force. See Siochru, Sean and Girard, Bruce. 2002. *Global Media Governance.* Lanham, Md.: Rowman and Littlefield.

12. Kuzmyk, Jenn. 1999. "Blinded by science," *RealScreen*, November, 36.

13. *Ibid.*

14. Saunders, Doug. 2001. "Hollywood goes to bat for nation," *Globe and Mail*, 19, A.

15. See Winston, Brian. 2000. *Lies, Damn Lies and Documentary.* London: British Film Institute.

16. Interview with Chris Haws, Discovery Channel, 18 October 2001.

17. Interview with Philip Hampson, 20 July 2001.

18. Tom Gardam cited in Fry, Andy. 1999. "Survival of the Fittest," *RealScreen*, December, 28.

19. According to Houle et al., Canada's documentary industry suffers from "insufficient consolidation." There are now well over three hundred producers working in the country. See Houle, Michel. 2000. *Documentary Production in Quebec and Canada 1991.2-1998/9: Phase 1,* www.ridm.qc.ca.

20. Interview with Chris Haws, Discovery Channel, 18 October 2001.

21. Scoffield, Heather. 2001. "Broadcasters seeking programming money," *Globe and Mail*, 25 October, B.

22. Goodman, Robert M. 2000. "Is Content King?" *Independent*, November, 38–39.

23. Monopoly integration has been partly kept in check in France, where Vivendi has been forced to divest its holdings in Canal Plus because of ownership laws. See Cowern, Christine. 2001. "Digital in France," *RealScreen*, June, 41.

24. Armstrong, Mary Ellen. 1998. "Editorial," *RealScreen*, May, 2.

25. Roberts, Bill. 2001. "Media mergers: more is less," *Globe and Mail*, 15 January, A.

26. Damsell, Keith. 2000. "CRTC seeks input on cable TV," *Globe and Mail*, 9 December, B.

27. Catherine Lamour, Canal Plus, cited in Clarke, Stephen. 1998. "Tribute to Catherine Lamour," *RealScreen*, April, 45.

28. Bob Wise, Discovery Channel producer, cited in Christie, Brendan. 1998. "Production conspiracy theories," *RealScreen*, June, 15.

29. Guy, Malcolm and Wintonick, Peter. 1998. "Policy notes," *POV*, fall, 9.

30. Canadian Television Fund (CTF). 1999. *Documentary Programming Module 1999*. Ottawa: CTF, 7. Extra merit points are also awarded to firms that are able to secure network license fees above and beyond the minimum 15 percent of their production budgets. Again, "connected" producers tend to benefit from these rules.

31. "Australia favours experienced producers," 1999, *Docos*, 17 July.

32. Saunders, Doug. 1997. "Exporting Canadian Culture," *Globe and Mail*, 25 January, C.

33. Perlmutter, Tom. 1993. "Distress Signals," in Tony Dowmunt (ed.) *Channels of Resistance*. London: British Film Institute.

34. "EU investigates BBC/Flextech deal," 2000, *Docos*, 17 October, 1.

35. The system still has a long way to go, however. At present users can browse samples of the collection and arrange for electronic delivery. The Bank, a subsidiary of Eastman Kodak, has acquired the archives of Visnews and British Paramount Newsreels due to its partnership with Reuters, and claims to offer more than one hundred years of footage from around the world.

36. "Documentary shop opens on-line," 1999, *Docos*, 3 January, 3.

37. Christie, Brendan. 1998. "The difference between rights and wrongs," *RealScreen*, March, 37.

38. Christie, Brendan. 1998. "Stock shots: World Images turns green," *RealScreen*, December, 20.

39. Christie, Brendan. 2000. "Taking stock of the web," *RealScreen*, July, 41. Predictably, subjects have fewer rights than owners when it comes to documentary footage. Standard release forms for globally circulating shows allow producers to use images "in perpetuity throughout the world" without hindrance from the people being

filmed. Keenlyside, Sarah. 2000. "Please release me," *RealScreen*, October, 56.

40. *Ibid*. Archivists themselves sometimes aid and abet hoarding. One admitted that "everything is a matter of money—if someone is going to pay me a rate that gives me the incentive to take [footage] off the market . . . for the terms of the contract, I'll do it." Joe Lavro cited in Christie, Brendan. 1998. "The difference between rights and wrongs," *RealScreen*, March, 37.

41. Though NGC insists "the findings are public domain. Anybody can do the story but not necessarily with that scientist." Larry Engle cited in Brown, Kimberley. 2000. "Buying science," *RealScreen*, December, 60.

42. Bouw, Brenda. 2001. "Taliban destroying Afghan film archives," *Financial Post*, 4 May, C.

43. Says one producer of digital discarding, "Our history is vanishing as we speak . . . if we don't have testimonials of what happened, then that history simply doesn't exist." Anonymously cited in Christie, Brendan. 1998. "Stock shots: World Images turns green," *RealScreen*, December, 20. Public archives often make matters worse, taking advantage of a "valuable resource heading into the 21st century," says Jeffrey Hopkinson, a librarian at the cash-strapped Canadian Broadcasting Corporation. Hopkinson cited in Christie, Brendan. 1997. "Special report on taking stock," *RealScreen*, October, 18. An official at France's Institut National de l'Audiovisuel adds that public archives are now ready to "compete in an international market in the midst of a technological revolution." "France's INA appoints head of archive sales," *Docos*, 20 June 2000. Digitalization, in this case, involves saving footage based on cost and profit calculations—at the expense of the public domain.

44. Archivist R. Berman-Bogdan cited in Christie, Brendan. 1998. "The difference between rights and wrongs," *RealScreen*, March, 37.

45. Blumenthal, Howard and Oliver Goodenough. 1998. *The Business of Television*. 2d ed. New York: Billboard Books.

46. Christie, Brendan. 1998. "The difference between rights and wrongs," *RealScreen*, March, 37.

47. Department of Culture, Media, and Sport, United Kingdom. 1999. *Report of the Creative Industries Task Force Report into Television Exports*, 52.

48. Keenlyside, Sarah. 2000. "The Future of footage," *RealScreen*, February, 39.

49. Christie, Brendan. 1998. "Stock shots: World Images turns green," *RealScreen*, December, 20.

50. Interview with Philip Hampson, 20 July 2001.

51. R. Berman-Bogdan cited in Christie, Brendan. 1998. "The difference between rights and wrongs," *RealScreen*, March, 37.

52. See Rayman, Susan. 2001. "The Trendspotting," *RealScreen*, March, 32.

53. See Vista Advisers for RAI. 2001. *The Documentary Market Worldwide*. Rome: RAI, 42.

54. See Houle, Michel. 2000. *Documentary Production in Quebec and Canada 1991.2–1998/9: Phase 1*, www.ridm.qc.ca.

55. Jacobsen, Ulla. 2000. "Bad news from independent countries," *Dox*, August, 30.

56. HBO documentary programming director cited in Kirchdoerffer, Ed. 1998. "Flash, cash and the ratings dash," *RealScreen*, September, 33.

57. Interview with Chris Haws, Discovery Channel, 18 October 2001.

58. *Ibid.*

59. Heather McAndrew cited in Hughes, Nancy. 1998. "Producer profiles: Asterisk Productions," *RealScreen*, August, 22.

60. Rayman, Susan. 2000. "Are distribs getting more for less," *RealScreen*, March, 56.

61. Anonymous producer cited in Kott, Michael. 1998. "Co-productions in full swing" *Playback*, 10 March, 5.

62. Dovey, Jon. 2000. *Freakshow: First Person Media and Factual Television*. London: Pluto Press, 151.

63. Zimmermann, Patricia. 2000. *States of Emergency: Documentaries, Wars and Democracies*. Minneapolis: University of Minnesota, 25.

64. Robins, Kevin. 1996. *Into the Image: Culture and Politics in the Field of Vision*. London: Routledge, 80.

65. See Barsam, R. 1974. "Defining non-fiction film," in Mast, G. and Cohen, M. (eds.), *Film Theory and Film Criticism*. New York: Oxford University Press, 366.

66. McLuhan, Marshall and Fiore, Quentin. 1967. *The Medium Is the Message*. Hammondsworth, England: Penguin, 16.

67. Bauman, Zygmunt. 1998. *Globalization: The Human Consequences*. New York: Columbia University Press, 92–93; and Bauman, Zygmunt. 1993. *Postmodern Ethics*, Oxford, England: Blackwell, 218.

68. See the report by the Third World and Environment Broadcasting Trust at www.ePolitix.com/EN/forums. This study covers the period leading up to but not including the attacks of September 11, 2001. It found that many "searching examinations" of cultures and social issues were quickly superseded in the aftermath by entertainment and "brochure" programs.

69. The science, arts, and educational categories account for 57 percent of distributor offerings and 60 percent of producer portfolios, according to a recent MIPDOC report. See Rayman, Susan. 2001. "The Trendspotting," *RealScreen*, March, 32.

70. For a critique of ARTE's pedagogical approach see Richardson, Kay and Meinhof, Ulrike A. 1999. *Worlds in Common: Television Discourse in a Changing Europe*. London: Routledge.

71. For a defense of scandal sheets on these grounds see Tomlinson, John. 1997. "And besides the wench is dead," in Lull, James and Hinerman, Stephen (eds.) *Media Scandals: Morality and Desire in the Popular Culture Marketplace*. New York: Columbia University Press, 65–84.

72. Stevenson, Nick. 1999. *The Transformation of the Media: Globalisation, Morality, and Ethics*. London: Longman, 132.

73. Sociologist Igor Kafanilov has noted that a "Russian can look at a [local reality] show like Road Patrol and think 'well, at least that terrible thing happened to the other guy and not to me'." But, typically, no actual viewer is cited in this report. Cited in Honore, Carl. 2000. "Russian TV becomes daily gore fest," *National Post*, 9 February, A.

74. "ABC cuts factual, demands extra funds," 2000, *DocTV*, 27 October, 4.

75. Jordan, Raphael. 2001. "Bona fide Brazil," *RealScreen*, October, 44.

76. Christie, Brendan. 2001. "Soldiering on," *RealScreen*, May, 6.

77. "BBC issues self-critical Annual Report," 2000, *DocTV*, 16 April.

78. Clarke, Steve. 2001. "Finding Eire time for documentaries," *RealScreen*, September, 32.

79. Vista Advisers for RAI. 2001. *The Documentary Market Worldwide*. Rome: RAI, 43.

80. The networks, however, are being given a run for their money in both countries by the specialty channels. See, for instance, Crawley, William. 1999. Introduction, *Media Asia* 26, (2): 81–89; and Houle, Michel. 2000. *Documentary Production in Quebec and Canada 1991/2-1998/9: Phase 1*, www.ridm.qc.ca.

81. EBU Chair Axel Arno cited in Hazan, Jenny. 2001. "The EBU," *RealScreen*, July, 21.

82. Moreover, the 1995 merger of the Scandinavian Broadcasting System with Central European Media Enterprises, forming the third-largest program buyer in the world, suggests that the project is succeeding to a degree. The merger pools the resources of eighteen channels in twelve countries, many of which could not produce, let alone export, their own documentaries. See "In brief," *RealScreen*, May, 6.

83. A 1998 deal between DNI and the BBC had the former investing more than $US660 million in coproductions and cross-promotions with the public service network. See Kirchdoerffer, Ed. 1998. "Upfront," *RealScreen*, April, 6. A more modest agreement between DNI and German broadcaster ZDF gave the latter access to the Discovery archives and DNI access to ZDF productions. See "ZDF and Discovery go public in co-pro and acquisition pact," 2000, *Docos.com*, 21 November.

84. See "German doc channel gets go-ahead," 1999, *DocTV*, 6 March, 2; and "BBC may move to genre-based channels," 1999, *Docos.com*, 14 July.

85. Frank, Steven. 2000. "History with a bang," *Time*, 23 October, 56. That series was actually designed as a "corrective" to the global image market. CPH would allow Canadians to "tell their own stories and not leave them up to the [American] A&E Network," according to the show's executive producer.

86. Mark Starowicz cited in Wisebord, Marilyn. 1997. "The Banff TV Festival," *POV*, summer/fall, 28.

87. Saunders, Doug. 1997. "Exporting Canadian Culture," *Globe and Mail*, 25 January, C.

88. Mark Starowicz cited in Wisebord, Marilyn. 1997. "The Banff TV Festival," *POV*, summer/fall, 28.

89. Houle, Michel. 2000. *Documentary Production in Quebec and Canada 1991.2-1998/9: Phase 1*, www.ridm.qc.ca.

90. Canadian Broadcasting Corporation (CBC). 1999. *Rough Cuts Guidelines*. Toronto: CBC, 1.

91. Martyn Burke, 1996. " 'Burial Ground': Stillborn at the CBC," *Globe and Mail*, 24 August, D.

92. The protest against the CBC's reediting of a point-of-view program concerning Mohawk Indian protests was only one example of the growing dissatisfaction with traditional documentary programming practices in the early 1990s. See Burgess, Diane. 2000. "Kanehsetake on Witness: The Evolution of CBC Balance Policy," *Canadian Journal of Communication* 25: 230–231.

93. See www.bbc.co.uk/info.

94. Independent Television Commission (ITC). 2001. *Programme Code*. London: ITC, 22.

95. Australian Broadcasting Corporation (ABC). 1994. *Editorial Policies*. Sydney: ABC, 10.

96. Crawley, William. 1999. Introduction, *Media Asia* 26 (2): 81–89.

97. Christie, Brendan. 1998. "The ABC's of PBS," *RealScreen*, February, 24.

98. Bullert, B.J. 1997. *Public Television: Politics in the Battle over Documentary.* New Brunswick, N.J.: Rutgers University Press.

99. Fry, Andy. 1998. "Broadcaster Profiles: Channel 4's Steve Howlett," *RealScreen*, March, 20.

100. Interview with Philip Hampson, 30 October 2001. Commissioning Editor Sara Ramsden responds that Channel 4 "hasn't got a duty to transmit [environmental messages]" that have "been seen before." Cited in Cowern, Christine. 1999. "Natural history vs. the environment," *RealScreen*, August, 24.

101. TVE's Robert Lamb cited in Fry, Andy. 1998. "TVE aims to make a difference rather than a profit," *RealScreen*, October, 36.

102. *Ibid.* ZDF's Horst Mueller makes the same point about environmental documentaries in Cowern, Christine. 1999. "Natural history vs. the environment," *RealScreen*, August, 24.

103. See www.amnesty.nl/filmfestival.

104. See Special Broadcasting Service (SBS). 1991. *Vision Statement,* www.sbs.com.au, Sydney.

105. See Special Broadcasting Service (SBS). 1999. *Codes of Practice,* 11, at www.sbs.com.au, Sydney; and Roscoe, who describes SBS as the "key documentary broadcaster in Australia," in Roscoe, Jane. 2001. "Australian documentary: Safe in the hands of the next generation," *Dox*, August, 11–13.

106. Cowern, Christine. 1999. "Canada's multi-faith network redefines nonprofit," *RealScreen*, February, 32.

107. Vision Television's Bill Roberts cited in Doyle, John. 2001. "A Vision of liberation from the shopping channel," *Globe and Mail,* 17 April, R.

108. Jan Rofenkamp cited in Fraser, Nick. 2004. "Odds and sods," *RealScreen*, August, 42.

109. Interview with Mary Ellen Davis, 13 October 2002.

110. *Ibid.*

Chapter 5

1. Rojek, Chris. 1997. "Indexing, dragging and the social construction of tourist sights," in Rojek, Chris and Urry, John (eds.), *Touring Cultures.* London: Routledge, 69.

2. Richardson, Kay and Meinhof, Ulrike A. 1999. *Worlds in Common: Television Discourse in a Changing Europe.* London: Routledge, 106.

3. Featherstone, Mike. 1991. *Consumer Culture and Postmodernism.* London: Sage, 5

4. "Animal magnetism the force in doc deals," 1997, *Playback*, 10 March, 21. Nature producers also work to "future proof" their shows by avoiding topical references.

5. Hibberd, Matthew, Kilborn, Richard, McNair, Brian, Marriott, Stephanie and Schlesinger, Philip. 2000. *Consenting Adults*. London: Broadcast Standards Council, 8.

6. Kuzmyk, Jenn. 1998. "MIP-Asia: Fighting the flu," *RealScreen*, December, 44.

7. See Hogarth, David. 2002. *Documentary Television in Canada: From National Public Service to Global Marketplace*. Montreal: McGill-Queens University Press, especially chapters 3 and 4.

8. Andrew Buchanan cited in Clarke, Steve. 1998. "Natural History," *RealScreen*, January, 30.

9. Anonymous producer cited in Christie, Brendan. 1997. "Special Report on Travel and Adventure," *RealScreen*, November, 34.

10. Cowern. Christine. 1999. "Re-creating history," *RealScreen*, November, 17.

11. Frank, Steven. 2000. "History with a bang," *Time*, 23 October, 56.

12. Rayman, Susan. 2000. "Still Life: Finding ways to bring 2-D images to life," *RealScreen*, October, 17. This is usually done, however, according to established notions of realism. Producers generally avoid effects that are "jarring and disruptive to the flow of the program." One producer says he uses "the same shots and edits" that he would with undoctored footage so "the camera work [never] stops the story." See Ed Joyce cited in *ibid*.

13. Rayman, Susan. 1999. "The color of stock," *RealScreen*, November, 56.

14. David Flitton cited in *ibid*.

15. Mrozek, Carl. 1999. "US HD post pioneers," *RealScreen*, October, 56.

16. "New trends," *Television Business International*, March 2000, 26.

17. Tertius. 1999. "Subjects and objects," *Globe and Mail*, 28 December, R.

18. Marjorie Kaplan cited in Brown, Kimberley. 2001. "'S' is for science," *RealScreen*, October, 95.

19. Anonymous producer cited in Kirchdoerffer, Ed. 1998. "Close up on Hollywood," *RealScreen*, January, 49.

20. March, Catherine Dawson. 2001. "The critical list," *Globe Television*, 28 July–3 August, 6.

21. Michael Apted cited in Hutcheson, Dawn. 1999. "Legitimacy Crisis," *RealScreen*, December, 11.

22. March, Catherine Dawson. 2001. "The Critical List," *Globe Television*, 28 July–3 August, 6.

23. Fry, Andy. 1998. "Upfront," *RealScreen*, March, 4. Of course, one kind of mixing can lead to another. HBO Vice President Sheila Nevins recalls that her early documentaries tackled topics like "Winston Churchill in a hot tub . . . then I thought I can't just do hot tubs, so maybe I can do a balancing act between highbrow and lowbrow." Cited in Thomson, Patricia. 2001. "Sheila's gotta have it," *Independent*, August/September, 33.

24. Igor Kafanilov cited in Honore, Carl. 2000. "Russian TV becomes daily gore fest," *National Post*, 9 February, A.

25. Oliver, Mary-Beth and Armstrong, G. Blake. 1995. *Journalism and Mass Communication Quarterly* 72 (3): 559–570.

26. Cowie, Elizabeth. 1999. "The spectacle of actuality," in Gaines, Jane M. and Renov, Michael (eds.), *Collecting Visible Evidence*. Minneapolis: University of Minnesota Press: 19–45.

27. Cited in Karen Voss. 2000. "The real deal," *Independent*, April, 33. For the reaction in other countries see "Portugal follows France in critique of reality shows," 2001, *Docos.com*, 29 May.

28. Cited in Karen Voss. 2000. "The real deal," *Independent*, April, 33.

29. Interview with Jeanne Neimi, 24 October 2001.

30. See Bird, S. Elizabeth. 2000. "Audience Demands in a Murderous Market," in Sparks, Colin and Tulloch, John (eds.), *Tabloid Tales: Global Debates over Media Standards*. Lanham, Md.: Rowman and Littlefield, 222–233. Bird's study, however, was based on just twenty-five subjects who filled out formal questionnaires with respect to three American shows.

31. Richardson, Kay and Meinhof, Ulrike. 1999. *Worlds in Common: Television Discourse in a Changing Europe*. London: Routledge, 7.

32. Kilborn, Richard. 2001. "Sign here please," *Dox*, December, 17.

33. Adamson, Rondi. 2001. "Still hooked and feeling no shame," *Globe and Mail*, 23 February, R.

34. See particularly the www.survivorsux.com and www.big brothersux.com sites.

35. Hibberd, Matthew, Kilborn, Richard, McNair, Brian, Marriott, Stephanie and Schlesinger, Philip. 2000. *Consenting Adults*. London: Broadcast Standards Council; and Syvertsen, Trine. 2001. "Ordinary people in extraordinary circumstances: a study of participants in television dating games," *Media, Culture and Society* 23 (4): 319–337. For subject reticence in North America see "On the Island, but in the closet," 2000, *Globe and Mail*, 23 August, R.

36. Australian Broadcasting Corporation. "Reality or Factual Format Television," online transcript, Radio National, *The Media Report*, 27 July 2000. Another critic's assertion that "younger viewers understand the reconstructive techniques of reality shows" because of their familiarity with home video and the genre itself is worth testing against assertions to the contrary. See "Docusoap: Truth or dare?" *Sight and Sound* 8 (4): 33.

37. Young, Patricia. 2000. "Heat, leaches and team spirit," *Globe and Mail*, 30 August, R.

38. "Survivin' for dollars," 2001, *Globe Television*, 16–21 October, 5. Protesters have taken MTV's *Real World* to task for the gentrification it has brought to their neighborhood, while Belizeans have complained of the unsavory image *Temptation Island* has given their country.

39. Doyle, John. 2000. "British fluff no contest for pioneer series," *Globe and Mail*, 17 November, R.

40. The *New York Times* describes *Frontier House* as reality television "in true public television style" and praises its "enlightenment" approach. See Rutenburg, Jim. 2000. "Manifest destiny," *New York Times*, 29 November, E.

41. Australian Broadcasting Corporation. 2000. "Reality or Factual Format Television," online transcript, Radio National, *The Media Report*, 27 July.

42. Murphy, John M. 1996. *Branding: A Key Marketing Tool*, New York: McGraw-Hill, 3.

43. Kirchdoerffer, Ed. 1999. "The truth about home video," *RealScreen*, July, 60.

44. Sponagle, Michael. 2001. "Brain pleaser," *Globe Television*, 5–11 May, 4.

45. "The danger we face," says this company programming official, "is trying to do too much." Instead, Discovery offers new channels while trying to ensure a predictable flow of audiences between them. Kirchdoerffer, Ed. 1999. "The truth about home video," *RealScreen*, July, 60.

46. Jennifer Hyde, commissioning editor at CNN, speaking at a pitch session, Hot Docs 1998 festival, Toronto, 20 March 1998.

47. Amy Briamonte, commissioning editor at A&E, speaking at a pitch session, Hot Docs 1998 festival, Toronto, 20 March 1998.

48. Ellis, John. 2000. "Scheduling: The last creative act in television," *Media, Culture and Society* 22 (2): 23.

49. Brown, Kimberley. 2000. "It's all just history repeating," *RealScreen*, December, 40.

50. Interview with Chris Haws, Discovery Channel, 18 October 2001.

51. Cited in Australian Broadcasting Corporation. 2000. "Reality or Factual Format Television," online transcript, Radio National, *The Media Report*, 27 July.

52. Burton Jablin of the Home and Garden Television Channel says his "investigative reports" can be enjoyed "just for the beautiful people you meet, or . . . for the information." "Upfront," 1999, *RealScreen*, May, 6.

53. Kuszmyk, Jenn. 1999. "Documall.com: Docs via e-commerce," *RealScreen*, May, 23–24.

54. Johnson, Tom. 1999. "More than One Way to See 'Content,'" *RealScreen*, May, 60. Digitalization may also allow for more backup texts to help viewers make sense of the programs. According to Charles Humbard, vice president and general manager of Discovery Communications, digitalized documentary programming will "make it much more plausible to realize multiple products for a project . . . everything from DVD's to books," Cited in Mrozek, Carl. 1998. "Technology: Nature in high definition," *RealScreen*, August, 26.

55. Rayman, Susan. 1999. "Undercover stock," *RealScreen*, July, 25.

56. Christie, Brendan. 1998. "Overview: Surveying the landscape," *RealScreen*, August, 6.

57. Australian Broadcasting Corporation (ABC). 1998. *Editorial Policies*. Sydney: ABC Corporate Affairs, 11.

58. For more about reenactments in public service programming see Hogarth, David. 2002. *Documentary Television in Canada: From National Public Service to Global Marketplace*. Montreal: McGill-Queens University Press, especially chapters 2 and 3 concerning what is sometimes referred to as the "Golden Age" of Canadian documentary television and radio. Many producers saw audiovisual effects to be the greatest achievement of Canadian broadcast documentaries.

59. Dickey, Christopher and Peyser, Mark. 2000. "CBS tries a Dutch treat," *Newsweek*, 10 July, 61.

60. Winston, Brian. 2000. *Lies, Damn Lies and Documentaries*. London: British Film Institute. See also BBC's *Producer Guidelines*, particularly chapters 2 and 7 on staging and re-creating events, at www.bbc.co.uk.

61. Australian Broadcasting Corporation (ABC). 1998. *Editorial Policies*. Sydney: ABC Corporate Affairs.

62. "French broadcasters reprimanded over fakes," 1999, *Docos .com*, 6 March.

63. Mark Samuels cited in Zeller, Susan. 2001. "Uprooting History," *RealScreen*, October, 7.

64. *Ibid.*

65. Dick, Ernest. 1994. "History on Television," *Archivaria* 34 (summer): 215.

66. Australian Broadcasting Corporation (ABC). 1998. *Editorial Policies.* Sydney: ABC Corporate Affairs, 11.

67. Margaret Dain cited in Cowern, Christine. 1999. "Re-creating history," *RealScreen*, November, 49.

68. *Ibid.*

69. Interview with Michael Resnick, 3 November 2001.

70. Cowern, Christine. 1999. "Re-creating history," *RealScreen*, November, 49.

71. Doyle, John. 2000. "British fluff no contest for pioneer series," *Globe and Mail*, 17 November, R.

72. Rayman, Susan. 1999. "The color of stock," *RealScreen*, November, 56.

73. Cowern, Christine. 1999. "Re-creating history," *RealScreen*, November, 49.

74. Moran, James M. 1999. "A bone of contention: Documenting the prehistoric subject," in Gaines, Jane M. and Renov, Michael (eds.), *Collecting Visible Evidence.* Minneapolis: University of Minnesota Press, 255–273.

75. Computer generation shows no sign of taking over documentaries any time soon. While some producers admire digitalized pictures for their freshness, flexibility, and commercial potential, others worry that they have a short shelf life and limited credibility. Younger viewers familiar with new technologies often find the programs dated as soon as they are released, while scientists "love to dispute [virtual] models." Most producers thus seem to agree with an official at the United Kingdom's 4:2:2 production company that "if you can shoot it for real, there's no point trying to replicate." Peter Bailey cited in Brown, Kimberley. 2000. "Un-natural history," *RealScreen*, August, 36.

76. Brown, Kimberley. 2000. "Un-natural history," *RealScreen*, August, 36.

77. *Ibid.*

78. "Nonfiction to go," 2000, *RealScreen*, April, 32.

79. See Fry, Andy. 1999. "The Sound and the Furry," *RealScreen*, August, 56.

80. Swedish producer Bo Landin cited in Kennedy, John. 1998. "Producer profiles: Scandinature Films," *RealScreen*, August, 37.

81. See, for instance, producer Neville Morgan cited in Kirchdoerffer, Ed. 1998. "Close up on Hollywood," *RealScreen*, January, 49.

82. "Nonfiction to go," 2000, *RealScreen*, April, 32.

83. *Ibid.*

84. Lutz, Catherine A. and Collins, Jane L. 1994. *Reading National Geographic*. Chicago: University of Chicago Press, 94.

85. In its 1999 Annual Report, for instance, the BBC criticized the free and generally unlabeled use of simulated pictures in the best-selling (1998) program *Walking with Dinosaurs*.

86. PBS producer Fred Kaufman cited in Christie, Brendan. 1998. "Overview: Surveying the landscape," *RealScreen*, August, 6.

87. Clarke Bunting cited in Kirchdoerffer, Ed. 1999. "The Promotional Punch," *RealScreen*, September, 46.

88. Susan Campbell cited in *ibid.*

89. Cited in Clarke, Stephen. 1998. "Tribute to Catherine Lamour," *RealScreen*, April, 45.

90. Producer Barry Clark asserts, "You do not go into a project with the idea of creating a program, but with the idea of acquiring digital assets that can be repurposed across various platforms." Cited in Brown, Kimberley. 2000. "Selling the planet at a location near you," *RealScreen*, August, 24.

91. See www.cbs.com/primetime/survivor, 6 October 2001.

92. Burnett, Mark and Dugard, Martin. 2000. *Survivor: The Ultimate Game*. New York: TV Books, 12.

93. *Ibid.*, 202.

94. *Ibid.*, 12.

95. Burnett, Mark. 2001. *Survivor II: The Field Guide*. New York: TV Books, 55.

96. Burnett, Mark and Dugard, Martin. 2000. *Survivor: The Ultimate Game*. New York: TV Books, 160.

97. Burnett, Mark. 2001. *Survivor II: The Field Guide*. New York: TV Books, 32.

98. *Ibid.*, 33.

99. Burnett says the way he "planned to shoot Survivor bore more comparison, logistically, to a feature film than to any type of TV show." *Ibid.*, 150.

100. Burnett, Mark and Dugard, Martin. 2000. *Survivor: The Ultimate Game*. New York: TV Books, 54.

101. *Ibid.*, 10.

102. Burnett, Mark. 2001. *Survivor II: The Field Guide*. New York: TV Books, 9.

103. *Ibid.*, 150.

104. Burnett, Mark and Dugard, Martin. 2000. *Survivor: The Ultimate Game.* New York: TV Books, 54.

105. *Ibid.*, 15.

106. For a reading of *Survivor* as a sign of "episto-crisis" see Howland, Jake. 2000. "Survivor bites: American TV in the twilight of the twilight," *Now* (Toronto), 16–22 August, 12. According to Howland, *Survivor* proves there is "no such thing as unscripted life anymore."

107. Bourdieu, Pierre. 1984. *Distinction: A Social Critique of the Judgment of Taste.* Cambridge, Mass.: Harvard University Press.

108. Quotes are taken from CBS *Survivor IV*, episode 1, February 28, 2002.

109. Burnett, Mark. 2001. *Survivor II: The Field Guide.* New York: TV Books, 8.

Chapter 6

1. Larson, Gary O. 2000. "The broadband revolution," *Independent*, May, 17–19.

2. Keenlyside, Sarah. 2000. "Canal Plus takes financial hit," *RealScreen*, April, 23.

3. At www.banffcentre.ab.ca (5 June 2000).

4. Rayman, Susan. 1999. "The health front," *RealScreen*, October, 44.

5. "The failure of new media," *Economist*, 19 August 2000, 54.

6. Atkin, David. 2000. "Website gave 'Survivor' its legs," *Financial Post*, 25 August, C.

7. "Extreme and Oxygen in reality crossover," 2000, *Docos.com*, 11 December.

8. Christie, Brendan. 2001. "By the numbers," *RealScreen*, March, 38.

9. "BBC stops commissioning 'programmes,'" 2001, *Docos.com*, 26 March.

10. Christie, Brendan. 2001. "By the numbers," *RealScreen*, March, 38.

11. *Ibid.*

12. "The failure of new media," 2000, *Economist*, 19 August, 54.

13. CNN's Miguel Gareia cited in Rayman, Susan. 2000. "Brainstorming with the broadcasters," *RealScreen*, April, 78.

14. Discovery's Jeff Craig cited in *ibid.*

15. CNN's Miguel Gareia cited in *ibid.*

16. BBC's David Docherty cited in *ibid.*

17. Critics maintain that the BBC has used public funds to finance

its digital market ventures. But as of 2000, the BBC had only spent US$31.5 million on online projects compared with its annual US$1.6 billion investment in analog media services. *Ibid.*

18. PBS' John Hollar cited in *ibid.*

19. Discovery's Jeff Craig cited in *ibid.*

20. Hansell, Saul. 2000. "Television giants flop on the web," *National Post*, 15 August, C.

21. *Ibid.*

22. See Helen Wheatley's arguments to this effect about natural history programming in Wheatley, Helen. 2004. "The limits of television?: Natural history programming and the transformation of public service broadcasting," *European Journal of Cultural Studies* 7 (3): 325–339.

23. See Homes, Su. 2004. "But this time you choose: Approaching interactive audiences in reality television," *International Journal of Cultural Studies* 7 (2): 213–231.

24. See, for instance, Rayman, Susan. 1999. "The health front," *RealScreen*, October, 44.

25. Euser, Caroline and Faber, Nathalie. 2001. "Cut-n-paste," *POV*, summer, 34.

26. *Ibid.*

27. Robert Drew cited in Powers, Thom. 2000. "Docfest set to expand," *RealScreen*, July, 14.

28. Paget, Derek. 1998. *No Other Way to Tell It*. Manchester, England: Manchester University Press, 209–210.

29. See the service's Website, Documall.com.

30. Sella, Marshall. 2000. "The electronic fishbowl," *New York Times*, 21 May, VI.

31. For example, Patricia Zimmermann says the Internet "displaces individuality inscribed within intellectual property laws." See Zimmermann, Patricia. 2000. *States of Emergency: Documentaries, Wars and Democracies*. Minneapolis: University of Minnesota Press, 171.

32. Rownd, Rob. 2000. "Four templates for the future," *Independent*, January/February, 12–14.

33. See "PBS and ITVS launch Wal-Mart website," 2001, *Docos .com*, 5 May.

34. See, for instance, Scoffield, Heather. 2001. "Broadcasters seek programming money," *Globe and Mail*, 25 October, B. Consider as well the control of interactive television guides by monopolies like the U.S.-based Gemstar Corporation. See, for instance, "Meet the Bill Gates of television," in *U.S. News and World Report*, 7 August 2000, 5–51.

35. "Upfront: Nonfiction news," 1999, *RealScreen*, September, 6.

36. See Zimmermann, Patricia. 2000. *States of Emergency: Documentaries, Wars, Democracies.* Minneapolis: University of Minnesota Press, 175. Gibbs, Lisa. 2001. "MediaRights.org," *Independent*, March, 43.

37. *Ibid.*

38. Houpt, Simon. 2002. "United States freelancers win pay for electronic rights," *Globe Television*, 26 March.

39. *Ibid.*

40. See, for instance, "400 jobs cut at CNN," *Wall Street Journal*, 18 January 2001, 18.

41. Kirchodoerffer, Ed. 1999. "Digital play in the US of A," *RealScreen*, April, 71.

42. *Ibid.*

43. Cited in Jacobsen, Ulla. 2001. "Mad Mundo: Raising responsibility in a Mad world," *Dox*, August, 8.

44. www.madmundo.tv.com.

45. Cited in Jacobsen, Ulla. 2001. "Mad Mundo: Raising responsibility in a Mad world," *Dox*, August, 8.

46. *Ibid.*

47. Grossberg, Lawrence. *Dancing in Spite of Myself: Essays on Popular Culture.* 1997. Durham, N.C.: Duke University Press.

Selected
Bibliography

Appadurai, Arjun. 1996. *Modernity at Large.* Minneapolis: University of Minnesota Press.

Auguson, Preta, De Angelis, Maria and Mazzotti, Maria. 1996. *The Quest for Quality: Survey on Television Viewing Scheduling Worldwide.* Rome: RAI, General Secretariat of Prix Italia.

Australian Broadcast Authority (ABA). 2000. *Investigation into Expenditure Requirements for PAY-TV Documentary Channels.* Sydney: ABA.

Australian Film Commission/Film Finance Corporation. 1999. *Report on the Film and Television Production Industry.* Sydney: Minister of the Arts and Centenary Federation.

Australian Film Finance Corporation (AFFC). 2002. *Investment Guidelines 2001/2.* Sydney: AFFC.

Australian Film Finance Corporation and Australian Film Commission. 2000. *Submission to the Australian Broadcasting Authority, Investigation into Expenditure Requirements for the PAY-TV Documentary Channels.* Sydney: ABA.

Barker, Chris. 1997. *Global Television: An Introduction.* Oxford, England: Blackwell.

Barsam, R. 1974. "Defining non-fiction film." In Mast, G. and Cohen, M. (eds.). *Film Theory and Film Criticism.* New York: Oxford University Press.

Bauman, Zygmunt. 1993. *Postmodern Ethics.* Oxford, England: Blackwell.

Bauman, Zygmunt. 1995. *Life in Fragments.* Oxford, England: Blackwell.

Bauman, Zygmunt. 1998. *Globalization: The Human Consequences.* New York: Columbia University Press.

Berland, Jody. 1993. "Sounds, image and social space: Music video and media reconstruction." In Frith, Simon, Goodwin, Andrew and

Grossberg, Lawrence (eds.). *Sound and Vision: The Music Video Reader*. London: Routledge.

Bird, Elizabeth. 2000. "Audience demands in a murderous market." In Sparks, Colin and Tulloch, John (eds.). *Tabloid Tales: Global Debates over Media Standards*. Lanham, Md.: Rowman and Littlefield, 222–233.

Blumenthal, Howard J. and Goodenough, Oliver. 1998. *The Business of Television*. 2d ed. New York: Billboard Books.

Bourdieu, Pierre. 1984. *Distinction: A Social Critique of the Judgment of Taste*. Cambridge, Mass.: Harvard University Press.

Bouse, Derek. 1998. "Are wildlife films really 'nature documentaries'?" *Critical Studies in Mass Communication* 15, no. 2 (June): 116–140.

Bruzzi, Stella. 2000. *New Documentary: A Critical Introduction*. London: Routledge.

Bullert, B.J. 1997. *Public Television: Politics in the Battle over Documentary*. New Brunswick, N.J.: Rutgers University Press.

Burgess, Diane. 2000. "Kanehsetake on Witness: The evolution of CBC balance policy." *Canadian Journal of Communication* 25: 231–230.

Burnett, Mark. 2001. *Survivor II: The Field Guide*. New York: TV Books.

Burnett, Mark and Dugard, Martin. 2000. *Survivor: The Ultimate Game*. New York: TV Books.

Canada. 1951. *Report of the Royal Commission on National Development in the Arts, Letters, and Sciences (Massey-Levesque)*. Ottawa: King's Printer.

Canadian Radio-television and Telecommunications Commission (CRTC). 2000. *Public Notice*. Ottawa: CRTC.

Canadian Television Fund (CTF). 1999. *Documentary Programming Module 1999*. Ottawa: CTF.

Canadian Television Fund (CTF). 2001. *Documentary Programming Module, 2000–2001*. Ottawa: CTF.

Christie, Brendan. 1998. "The difference between rights and wrongs." *RealScreen*, March, 37.

Cleasby, Adrian. 1995. *What in the World Is Going On? British Television and Global Affairs*. London: Third World and Environmental Broadcasting Project.

Cohen, Barri. 2000. *The Canadian Perspective: In Search of a Definition*. Toronto: Canadian Independent Film Caucus.

Corner, John. 1996. *The Art of Record*. Manchester, England: Manchester University Press.

Cowie, Elizabeth. 1999. "The spectacle of actuality." In Gaines, Jane M. and Renov, Michael (eds.). *Collecting Visible Evidence*. Minneapolis: University of Minnesota Press.

Curran, James. 1999. "The crisis of public communication: A re-appraisal." In Liebes, Tamar and Curran, James (eds.). *Media, Ritual and Identity*. London: Routledge.

Curtin, Michael. 1993. *Redeeming the Wasteland: Television Documentary and Cold War Politics*. New Brunswick, N.J.: Rutgers University Press.

Dauncey, Hugh. 1996. "French reality television: More than a matter of taste." *European Journal of Communication* 11 (1): 81–94.

David Graham and Associates. 2000. *British Television: The Global Market Challenge*. London: British Television Directors Association.

David Graham and Associates. 2000. *Building a Global Audience: British Television in Overseas Markets*. Taunton, England: U.K. Department of Culture, Media and Sport.

David Graham and Associates. 2000. *Out of the Box: A Report for the Department of Culture, Media, and Sport*. Taunton, England: U.K. Department of Culture, Media and Sport.

Dolman, Trish. 2000. "The future of the documentary one-off." *Independent*, March, 35–37.

Dovey, Jon. 2000. *Freakshow: First Person Media and Factual Television*. London: Pluto Press.

During, Simon. 1997. "Popular culture on a global scale: A challenge for cultural studies?" *Critical Inquiry* 23 (summer): 809–831.

Ellis, John. 2000. "Scheduling: The last creative act in television." *Media, Culture and Society* 22 (2): 25–38.

Featherstone, Mike. 1991. *Consumer Culture and Postmodernism*. London: Sage.

Fishman, Jessica M. 1999. "The populace and the police in reality-based crime TV." *Critical Studies in Mass Communication* (16): 268–288.

Fishman, Mark and Calendar, Gary (eds.). 1998. *Entertaining Crime: Television Reality Programs*. New York: Aldine de Gruyter.

Fry, Andy. 1999. "Around the world in 3650 days." *RealScreen*, February, 74.

Gabori, Susan. 1979. "MIP-TV: Programming the world." *Cinema Canada*, August, 29–31.

Gaines, Jane M. 1999. "Introduction: The real returns." In Gaines, Jane M. and Renov, Michael (eds.). *Collecting Visible Evidence*. Minneapolis: University of Minnesota Press.

Glynn, K. 2000. *Tabloid Culture: Trash Taste, Popular Power, and the Transformation of American Television*. Durham, N.C.: Duke University Press.

Graham, David and Associates. *See* David Graham and Associates.

Grierson, John. 1979. *Grierson on Documentary*. London: Faber and Faber.

Grossberg, Lawrence. *Dancing in Spite of Myself: Essays on Popular Culture*. 1997. Durham, N.C.: Duke University Press.

Guattari, Felix. 1992. *Soft Subversions*. New York: Semiotext(e).

Hahn, Brigitte J. 1997. *Umerziehung durch Dokumentarfilm? ein Instrument amerikanischer Kulturpolitik im nach-Kriegsdeutschland (1945-1953)*. Munster, Germany: Lit.

Havens, Timothy. 2000. "The biggest show in the world: Race and the global popularity of the Cosby show." *Media, Culture and Society* 22 (4): 371–391.

Hazan, Jenny. 2001. "Getting global." *RealScreen*, March, 69.

Hibberd, Matthew, Kilborn, Richard, McNair, Brian, Marriott, Stephanie and Schlesinger, Philip. 2000. *Consenting Adults*. London: Broadcast Standards Council.

Hogarth, David. 2001. "Communication policy in a global age." In Burke, Mike, Mooers, Colin and Shields, John (eds.). *Restructuring and Resistance*. Toronto: Fernwood Press.

Hogarth, David. 2002. *Documentary Television in Canada: From National Public Service to Global Marketplace*. Montreal: McGill-Queens University Press.

Hoskins, Colin and McFadyen, Stuart. 1993. "Canadian participation in international co-productions and co-ventures in television programming." *Canadian Journal of Communication* 18 (fall): 219–236.

Houle, Michel. 2000. *Documentary Production in Quebec and Canada, 1991/2-1998/9: Phase 1*. www.ridm.qc.ca.

Independent Television Commission (ITC). 2001. *Programme Code*. London: ITC.

Izod, John, Kilborn, Richard and Hibberd, Matthew. 2000. *From Grierson to the Docu-Soap: Breaking the Boundaries*. Luton, England: University of Luton Press.

Jacobsen, Ulla. 2001. "Mad mundo: Raising responsibility in a Mad world." *Dox*, August, 8.

Keenlyside, Sarah. 2000. "Please release me." *RealScreen*, October, 56.

Kilborn, Richard. 1994. "How real can you get? Recent developments in reality television." *European Journal of Communication* 9 (3): 421–439.

Kilborn, Richard. 1996. "New contexts in documentary production in Britain." *Media, Culture and Society* (18): 141–150.

Kilborn, Richard. 2001. "Sign here please." *Dox*, December, 17–18.

Kilborn, Richard and Izod, John. 1999. *An Introduction to Television Documentary*. Manchester, England: Manchester University Press.

Kjeldsen, Klaus. 2001. "Docs in a kid's perspective." *Dox*, December, 21.

Koch, Eric. 1991. *Inside Seven Days*. Scarborough, Ontario: Prentice-Hall.

Kunothangan, Gladius D. 2000. "Media content in Asia: More waste or substance?" *Media Asia* 26 (3): 17.

Lash, S. and Urry, J. 1994. *Economies of Signs and Spaces*. London: Sage.

Leakey, Richard and Morell, Virginia. 2001. *Wildlife Wars: My Fight to Save Africa's Natural Treasures*. New York: St. Martin's Press.

Longfellow, Brenda. 1996. "Globalization and national identity in Canadian film." *Canadian Journal of Film Studies* 5, no. 2 (fall): 3–16.

Lutz, Catherine A. and Collins, Jane L. 1994. *Reading National Geographic*. Chicago: University of Chicago Press.

MacDonald, Kevin and Cousins, Mark (eds.). 1996. *Imagining Reality: The Faber Book of the Documentary*. London: Faber and Faber.

McChesney, R.W. and Herman, E.S. 1997. *The Global Media*. London: Cassell.

McGuigan, Jim. 1996. *Culture and the Public Sphere*. London: Routledge.

McLaughlin, Lisa. 1993. "Feminism, the public sphere, media and democracy." *Media, Culture and Society* 15 (3): 599–620.

McLuhan, Marshall and Fiore, Quentin. 1967. *The Medium Is the Message*. Hammondsworth, England: Penguin.

Miller, Toby, Govil, Nitin, McMurria, John and Maxwell, Richard. 2001. *Global Hollywood*. London: British Film Institute.

Moran, James M. 1999. "A bone of contention: Documenting the prehistoric subject." In Gaines, Jane M. and Renov, Michael (eds.). *Collecting Visible Evidence*. Minneapolis: University of Minnesota Press, 255–273.

Murphy, John M. 1996. *Branding: A Key Marketing Tool*. New York: McGraw-Hill.

Negus, Keith. 1999. *Music Genres and Corporate Culture*. London: Routledge.

New on the Air (NOTA). 2001. *Yearly Report*. www.e-nota.com/reports.

Oliver, Mary-Beth and Armstrong, G. Blake. 1995. *Journalism and Mass Communication Quarterly* 72 (3): 559–570.

Paget, Derek. 1998. *No Other Way to Tell It*. Manchester, England: Manchester University Press, 1998.

Perlmutter, Tom. 1993. "Distress signals." In Tony Dowmunt (ed.). *Channels of Resistance*. London: British Film Institute.

Public Broadcasting Service (PBS). 2001. Pacific Islanders in Communications guidelines. http://piccom.org.

Richardson, Kay and Meinhof, Ulrike A. 1999. *Worlds in Common: Television Discourse in a Changing Europe.* London: Routledge.

Robins, Kevin. 1996. *Into the Image: Culture and Politics in the Field of Vision.* London: Routledge.

Rojek, Chris. 1997. "Indexing, dragging and the social construction of tourist sights." In Rojek, Chris and Urry, John (eds.). *Touring Cultures.* London: Routledge, 69.

Roscoe, Jane. 2001. "Australian documentary: Safe in the hands of the next generation." *Dox,* August, 11–13.

Roscoe, Jane. 2004. "Television and Australian documentary." *Media, Culture and Society* 26 (2): 288.

Ryninks, Kees. 2002. "DocuZone: A Dutch digital experiment." *Dox,* April, 9.

Sassen, Saskia. 2001. In Appadurai, Arjun (ed.). *Globalization.* Durham, N.C.: Duke University Press.

Schlesinger, Philip and Tumbler, Howard. 1994. *Reporting Crime: The Media Politics of Criminal Justice.* Oxford, England: Clarendon Press.

Siochru, Sean and Girard, Bruce. 2002. *Global Media Governance.* Lanham, Md.: Rowman and Littlefield.

Sparks, Colin. 1998. "Is there a global public sphere?" In Thussu, Daya (ed.). *Electronic Empires: Global Media and Local Resistance.* London: Edward Arnold.

Special Broadcasting Service (SBS). 1991. *Vision Statement.* www.sbs.com.au. Sydney.

Special Broadcasting Service (SBS). 1999. *Codes of Practice.* www.sbs.com.au. Sydney.

Statistics Canada. 1998. *Tabulations of Documentaries 1995-7.* Ottawa: Minster of Supply and Services.

Steven, Peter. 1992. *Brink of Reality: New Canadian Documentary Film and Video.* Toronto: Between the Lines.

Stevenson, Nick. 1999. *The Transformation of the Media: Globalisation, Morality and Ethics.* London: Longman.

Television France International (TFI). 2001. *Synthèse des flux internationaux de la production française 2000.* Paris: TFI.

Thompson, John B. 1997. "Tradition and self in a mediated world." In Heelas, Paul, Lash, Scott and Morriset, Paul (eds.). *Detraditionalization: Critical Reflections on Authority and Identity.* Oxford, England: Blackwell.

Tomlinson, John. 1997. "And besides the wench is dead." In Lull, James and Hinerman, Stephen (eds.). *Media Scandals: Morality and De-*

sire in the Popular Culture Marketplace. New York: Columbia University Press.

Tomlinson, John. 1999. *Globalization and Culture.* Chicago: University of Chicago Press.

Verna, Tony. 1996. *Global Television: How to Create Effective Television for the Future.* London: Longman.

Vista Advisers for RAI. 2001. *The Documentary Market Worldwide.* Rome: RAI.

Waldman, Diane and Walker, Janet (eds.). 1999. *Feminism and Documentary.* Minneapolis: University of Minnesota Press.

Whitney, D. Charles, Wartella, Ellen, Lasorsa, Domenic and Danielson, Wayne. 1999. "Monitoring 'reality' television: The national television violence study." In Nordenstrong, Kaarle and Griffin, Michael (eds.). *International Media Monitoring.* Cresskill, N.J.: Hampton Press.

Williams, Mark. 1999. "History in a flash: Notes on the myth of TV liveness." In Gaines, Jane M. and Renov, Michael (eds.). *Collecting Visible Evidence.* Minneapolis: University of Minnesota Press.

Winston, Brian. 1995. *Claiming the Real: Griersonian Documentary and Its Legitimations.* London: British Film Institute.

Winston, Brian. 2000. *Lies, Damn Lies and Documentary.* London: British Film Institute.

Woodward, Leslie. 2000. "Documentary as a casualty of the ratings war." *DocTV,* 4 September, 2.

Zimmermann, Patricia R. 2000. *States of Emergency: Documentaries, Wars, Democracies.* Minneapolis: University of Minnesota Press.

Index

A&E (Arts and Entertainment
   Network), commissioning
   of documentaries, 28, 68,
   98, 105
Aesthetic reflexivity, 6
Africa
   depiction in documentaries,
      56–61
   share of documentary market,
      25
Africa, 56–61
Alliance-Atlantis, 69
Alpert, Jon, 132
American Experience, 108
*America's Funniest Home
   Videos*, 97
Amnesty International, 36
Amsterdam International Docu-
   mentary Festival, 33
Ancillary products, 165n50
Appadurai, Arjun, 11
Armstrong, Mary Ellen, 69
Arnait Productions, 32
ARTE Channel, 22, 138n12
Article Z, 131–134
Asia, share of global documen-
   tary market, 25
Associated Producers, 48
Asterisk Productions, 77
Australia

Australian Broadcasting Corporation, 26, 81
Australian Film Commission,
   36
Australian Film Finance Corporation, 25
Australian International
   Documentary Confer-
   ence, 36
co-productions, 45
definitions of documentary,
   144n47
documentary film production,
   138–139n12
factual verification rules,
   107–108
independent productions,
   70–71
license fees, 147n37
local content regulations,
   42–43
minority programming, 84
reality show participants, 102
share of global documentary
   market, 25–26
Axel, Arno, 32

Bank, The (Eastman Kodak),
   156n35
Barker, Chris, 13

Barrat, Patrice, 133
Battlefield, 95
Bauman, Zygmunt, 11, 20, 79
Bazalgette, Peter, 105
BBC (British Broadcasting Corporation)
  co-ventures, 10
  and Discovery Networks International, 71, 160n83
  early official coproductions, 29
  fairness and impartiality rules, 65–66
  importance of documentary programming, 7
  and independent producers, 70
  and minorities, 84
  Natural History Unit, 110
  reenactments, 165n60
  webcasts, 125–126, 155n11
Belize, 164n38
Big Brother
  audience appeal, 101
  local versions, 37, 38, 47
  websites, 103
Bird, Elizabeth, 163n30
Bowling for Columbine, 139n12
Brazil
  cuts in public service programming, 8
  depiction in documentaries, 131–134
  independent production, 28
British Columbia, 43
British Pathé, 72
Broomfield, Nick, 99
Bruzzi, Stella, 13
Bullert, B. J., 137n6
Bureau du film du Québec, 56
Burke, Martyn, 44–45
Burnett, Mark, 116, 120

Campaign for Quality Television, 98

Canada
  coproductions, 48
  corporate concentration, 155n19
  definitions of documentary, 144n47
  documentary archives, 157n43
  documentary imports, 26
  documentary exports, 30
  documentary websites, 108
  local content regulations, 43, 151n9
  reality program participants, 102
  reality program styles, 49
  reenactments, 109
Canada: A People's History
  as public service programming, 83, 140n20
  use of digital reenactments, 94–95
Canadian Television Fund, 42, 70, 156n30
Canal Plus, 70, 114
Castaway Productions, 38, 150n89
Castaway 2000, 103
CBC (Canadian Broadcasting Corporation)
  critics of, 160n92
  digital archives, 157n43
  early official coproductions, 30
  global market strategies, 82–84
  importance of documentaries on, 7, 139n16
CBS (Columbia Broadcasting System), 116
Censorship, examples in a global market, 63–67
Chains of Love, 102
Channel branding, 104

Channel 4
  and independent producers, 48
  and point-of-view program-
    ming, 85
China, documentary imports
  and exports, 27–28, 34
CNN (Cable News Network)
  digital strategies, 125
  foreign program purchases, 22
  importance of documentaries
    on, 124
Cold War, 128
Control Room, 87
Coproductions
  current importance, 31–33
  early examples, 29
  impact on local programming,
    44–46
Copyright
  restrictions on documentary
    programming, 71–74
  on the web, 130
Corporate concentration, in a
  global documentary market,
  67–71
Cowie, Elizabeth, 99
Cromwell Productions, 108

Davis, Mary-Ellen, 90
Dawn of the Eye, 83
Deep Dish TV, 86
Denmark, 39
D-Film, 35
Digital documentaries, 122–124
Digital simulation
  future of, 165n54
  in history programs, 166n75
  styles, 162n12
DNI (Discovery Networks Inter-
    national)
  Africa series, 56–60
  brand image, 104
  censorship, 64–65

children's programming, 96
and Chinese market, 27–28
coproductions, 10, 17, 21, 50–
    55, 71, 160n83
digital strategies, 126–127
exclusivity rules, 73
importance of documentaries
    on, 123–124
and independent producers,
    68, 70
social issue documentaries,
    76–77
theme nights, 105
truth value of programs, 113–
    114
Docudrama, as local program-
    ming, 47
Documall, 106, 129
Documania, 1
Documentary archives, 157n40
Documentary budgets, 30–31
Documentary definitions, 14–15,
    143–144n47, 144n49
Documentary films
  independent filmmaking,
    87–88
  origins and future of, 3–4,
    137–138n12
Documentary News Net, 72
Documentary participants,
    156–157n39
Documentary producers, as
    sources of information, 15,
    32
Documentary production
  in a broadcast market, 5
  in a consolidated market,
    69–70, 129–131
Documentary production statis-
    tics
  accuracy of, 19–20
  global statistics, 25–29, 145n2,
    145n4

Documentary texts
  in a broadcast market, 5–6
  in a global market, 76–78,
    99–101
Documentary viewing
  of reality programs, 99
  screening out, 79
  of television, 6
  of webcasts, 127–129, 163n30,
    164n36
Docusoaps
  declining demand for, 76
  as genre hybrid, 96, 98
  and local culture, 47
  participants in, 93
  as public service genre, 78
Docuzone, 138n12
Domestic documentaries, 21–24
Doordarshan, 54, 85
Dovey, Jon, 49, 78
Doyle, John, 102
DVD, 95

EBU (European Broadcasting
    Union)
  definition of documentaries,
    145n49
  funding of coproductions, 32,
    82
Eco-Challenge, 116
Empire State Building, 72
Encounters (film festival), 33
Endemol
  format disputes, 150n89
  and local production, 37, 38, 47
Ethical Risk Assessments, 66–67
Eurodoc, 47
European Community, 71
European Storytellers (film
    festival), 35

Fahrenheit 911, 87
Featherstone, Mike, 92

Feldman, Seth, 142n41
Festivals and markets, 33–36
fifth estate, the, 83
Fiore, Quentin, 78
Fishman, Jessica M., 143n46
Flaherty, Robert, 112
FOCAL (Federation of Com-
    mercial and Audiovisual
    Libraries), International, 23,
    146n26
Ford Motor Company, 132
Formats
  and copyright laws, 150n89
  importance in a global mar-
    ket, 36–39
  as local content, 46–47, 49
  local protests over, 49–50
France
  corporate concentration, 67
  documentary archives, 157n43
  documentary films, 138–
    139n12
  domestic funding, 147n31
  share of global documentary
    market, 25
FRAPA (Format Recognition and
    Property Association), 37
Free speech, international con-
    ventions on, 65
Frontier House, 103

Gaines, Jane, 142n39
GATS (General Agreement on
    Trade in Services), 68
Gemstar Corporation, 169n34
Generic footage, 93
Gilligan's Island, 116
Girard, Bruce, 155n11
Giros Productions, 31–32
Global Television Network, 47
Goodall, Jane, 57
Great North Communications,
    69

Greenpeace, 74
Grierson, John, 138n7
Griersonian documentaries, 80
Grifa, Fernando, 28
Guatemala, 88–90
Guattari, Felix, 6, 139n14

Hahn, Brigitte, 142n42
Hampson, Philip, 22–23
Hang the DJ, 56
Haunted Land, 88–90
Haws, Chris, 51
HBO (Home Box Office) net-
   work, 76, 138n12, 163n23
Hendricks, John, 51
Hibberd, Matthew, 13, 143n42
History Channel, 54, 68
History programs
   as local content, 49
   as public service program-
      ming, 83
   scheduling, 100
   use of reenactments, 94–95
History Television
   local formats, 49
   reenactments, 108
   scheduling, 100
Hogarth, David, 137n6, 165n58
Home and Garden Television
   channel, 165n52
Homogeneity of documentary
   programming, 75–76
Hong Kong International Film
   and Television Market, 33,
   34
Hot Docs Film Festival, 33, 35
Houle, Michel, 155n19
How Geraldo Lost His Job, 131–
   134

Independent Film and Documentary Channel, 69
Independent Film Project, 33

Indymedia Documentation
   Project, 86
Ingram, Jay, 57–60
INPUT (International Public
   Television Conference), 36,
   42
Institut National de l'Audio-
   visuel, 157n43
Interactive television, 169n34
Intermag program exchange, 29
International Documentary
   Association, 32, 36
International Documentary
   Source Book, 72
International Wildlife Film
   Festival, 74
Internet, 124–128
Intertel program exchange,
   29–30
Ireland
   documentary budget cuts, 81
   local content regulations, 43
Israel, 27
Izod, Keith, 143n42

Jablin, Burton, 165n52
Jane Balfour Productions, 68
Johnson, Tom, 106

Kafanilov, Igor, 99, 159n73
Kastner, John, 45
Kilborn, Richard, 13, 143n42,
   143n45
Kott, Michael, 45
Krasnagorsk archives, 72

Lamour, Catherine, 114
Lash, Scott, 137n2
Latin America, documentary
   imports and exports, 28, 77
Leakey, Richard, 57, 154n64
Levin, Gerald, 137n1
License fees, 77

Live broadcasting, 123–124
Loft Story, 50
Longfellow, Brenda, 13

Malaysia, 115
Maysles, Albert, 10
McDocumentaries, 1, 5, 76
McDonald's, 128–129
McLuhan, Marshall, 78
MediaRights.org, 130
Meinhof, Ulrike, 92
Menton, Barraclough Clarey, 69
Middle East
   censorship, 64
   share of global documentary market, 25
MIPDOC (Marché Internationales des Programmes Documentaires), 33, 125, 137n1
Mumbai International Film Festival, 35
Mundo Olé, 28

National Geographic Channel
   and Chinese market, 28
   digital strategies, 127
   exclusivity rules, 73
   local production policies, 54
NATPE (National Association of Television Program Executives), 34
Nature programs
   history of, 110
   as local programming, 153n62
   truth value, 110–114
   uniform style, 45–46
   use of footage, 93–94
NBC (National Broadcasting Corporation), 30
Negus, Keith, 154n68
Netherlands, 138n12

Nevins, Sheila, 163n23
Newman, Sidney, 3, 138n7
New Zealand, 42
NFB (National Film Board of Canada), 3
Norway, 102
NOTA (New on the Air) Report, 37
Noujaim, Jahane, 87

Odyssey Network, 54
Oliver, Mary Beth, 99
One World Television Service, 132
Osbournes, The, 96

Pacific Islanders in Communications, 42, 44
Paget, Derek, 47
Paper Tiger TV, 86
PBS (Public Broadcasting Service)
   early official coproductions, 29, 42, 82
   minority programming policies, 85
   webcasting, 125
Pioneer Quest, 49
Plague Monkeys, The, 45
Point–of–view documentaries, 76
Popstars, 39
Probst, Jeff, 116–119
Public service documentaries
   as alternative to the global market, 81–87, 217n6
   early international program exchanges, 29
   importance as public service programming, 139n16
   origins and aims, 3, 7
   share of global market, 24–25
Public sphere, global market possibilities, 62

REAL: Life on Film (film festival), 35
Reality programs
  as genre hybrid, 95–96
  and meaning, 98–99
  origins and growth, 37
  as trend in programming, 150n87
Real World, 164n38
Red Cross, 74
Reenactments, 106–109
Resnick, Michael, 108
Richardson, Kay, 92
Road Patrol, 99
Roberts, Bill, 69
Robins, Kevin, 78–79
Rojek, Chris, 92
Roscoe, Jane, 13, 161n105
Rough Cuts, 82–83
Rough Science, 98
RTÉ (Radio Telefís Éireann), 81
Russian Orthodox Church, 99

Saskatchewan Film and Video
  Development Corporation, 56
Sassen, Saskia, 39
Satellite broadcasting, 64
SBS (Special Broadcasting Service), 86, 161n105
Science documentaries, 66
Sheffield International Documentary Festival, 33
Siochru, Sean, 155n11
Sithengi Film Festival, 33
Specialty channels, importance in a global market, 32, 141n28, 159n80
Steven, Peter, 12–13
Stevenson, Nick, 80
Sundance Film Festival, 138n12
Sunny Side of the Doc (film festival), 33

Survivor
  criticisms of, 168n106
  local versions, 47, 101
  rights disputes, 38
  as text, 118–121
  truth value, 115–118
Survivor Films, 74

Taliban, 73
Taylor, Joyce, 51
Television
  future as a documentary medium, 123–128, 143n44
  impact on documentaries, 4–6
Television Business International, 95
Television Trust for the Environment, 85
Temptation Island, 103
Third Date, 98
Third World and Environment Broadcasting Trust, 158n68
Time Warner, 64
Titanic, 113, 123–124
Tomlinson, John, 159n71
TV Cultura, 81
TV Globo, 54
TVNewZealand, 22, 68

UNESCO, 47
United Kingdom
  airing of international documentaries, 22
  copyright laws, 74
  corporate concentration, 67
  documentary participants, 102
  factual verification rules, 107
  infotainment programming, 79
  point-of-view programming, 84–85
  share of global documentary market, 25
  television viewers, 101

United States
  copyright laws, 74
  definition of documentary,
    143–144n47
  documentary film, 138n12
  factual verification propa-
    ganda, 66, 148n55

Vatican Church, 99
Vision TV, 78, 86

Walking with Dinosaurs, 109
Wear, Don, 54
Webcasts, 124–128
Wheatley, Helen, 169n22
Whispered Media, 86

Winston, Brian, 13, 137n6,
  143n45
World Images, 74
World Journeys, 21
World Television, 22
World Union of Documentary,
  78
World War III, 108–109
WTO (World Trade Organiza-
  tion), 24, 47

ZDF (Zweites Deutsches
  Fernsehen), 81–82, 105,
  161n102
Zimmermann, Patricia, 13, 78,
  142n40, 170n36